TEXAS
THUNDER

TEXAS THUNDER

*My Eleven Years with
the Dallas Cowboys*

by

Harvey Martin

RAWSON ASSOCIATES : New York

Library of Congress Cataloging-in-Publication Data
Martin, Harvey.
Texas thunder.
Includes index.
1. Martin, Harvey. 2. Football players—United States—
Biography. 3. Dallas Cowboys (football team) I. Title.
GV939.M295A3 1986   796.332′092′4 [B]   85-43535
ISBN 0-89256-312-5

Published simultaneously in Canada by Collier Macmillan Canada, Inc.
Packaged by Rapid Transcript, a division of March Tenth, Inc.
Composition by Folio Graphics Co., Inc.
Manufactured by Fairfield Graphics, Fairfield, Pennsylvania
Designed by Jacques Chazaud
First Edition

To
my mother, Sharon Bell, Chase,
and God

ACKNOWLEDGMENTS

I want to thank Willie Mae Johnson, my aunt, who always made Christmas special; Mary, my sister; William Session; Patti Franklin; Corine Williams; Virgie Grant; Judy Hoffman; Preston Pearson; Lea, Ethan, and Micah Lewis; Charley Pride; Lynn Turner; Jim Rodgers; Bill Polson; Sidney Wren; Dwight White; Rayfield Wright; Terri Hoffman; Babs Holder; Debbie Hanover; Ilene Turkowitz, a very special lady; Biff Windsor; Ernie Stautner; Norman Jett; Boley Crawford; Ernest Hawkins; Michael Schutze; Chad Brown; Trammell Crow; Jack Evans, former mayor of Dallas; Mayor Starke Taylor of Dallas; Janie Tilford; John and Anita Reeves; Jill Lucas; Kathy Richards; Ronald and Susan Welborn; Mitchell Greenstein; Bonnie Ricca; Gene Fishel; Charles Ced; Betty Duke; Larry Sussman; Drew Pearson; Bob Lilly; D. D. Lewis; Ron Dubner, my attorney; Howard Weinberger; Buddy Gregory; Dave Godin; Walder Martins; Martin Marshall; All Hammons; Harold Abramson; and my dog, Lucifer.

TEXAS THUNDER

1

The huge crowd stood and roared its approval.

It was late November 1977, and I'd just slammed Philadelphia Eagles quarterback Ron Jaworski to the Texas Stadium Astroturf—my twenty-third sack of the season, breaking the Dallas Cowboys record held by George Andrie.

On the stadium scoreboard, in giant letters, blinked the word *MARTINIZED!* My trademark. It meant I'd demolished another high-paid quarterback.

When I pounded Jaworski to the ground the noise generated by the 60,289 fans was terrific. It became deafening when the public address announcer informed them I'd broken the record.

The referee stopped the game and gave me the ball. I stood in the center of the field, an athlete at the absolute peak of his ability, for opponents a frighteningly efficient, perfectly tuned, flawlessly operating *football machine.* This year I'd be honored as Defensive Most Valuable Player of the entire NFL.

I stood near midfield and held the ball aloft, the thunder of the big crowd in my ears—Texas thunder. Then I pointed the ball to the exact seats where I knew my girl friend, Sharon Bell, and my mom watched. Without them the delicious moment, so many delicious moments, wouldn't have been possible.

I listened to the crowd, letting its sound penetrate my pores, all the way to my soul, and marveled how totally implausible, impossible, all of this would have seemed just a few years before.

My thirteenth summer was the last I spent in its entirety with my grandfather, Mr. Buster, and my grandmother, Lucy Belle Britt. Until then, however, I hadn't missed a one. For my sister, Mary, and me, spending our summers in Mabank (pronounced *May*bank), Texas, seventy-five miles southeast of Dallas, was as regular as the seasons. My mom took me and Mary, a year younger than I, to the town of 922 during the first week of June and picked us up around Labor Day. Mary and I loved staying with our grandparents (they spoiled us shamelessly), and Mom and Dad believed the atmosphere of a small town more wholesome than the troubled sidewalks of Dallas.

Mr. Buster and Lucy Belle had a good-sized home in Mabank, a tribute to their willingness to work from early morning to late at night. There was a big front lawn with two huge oak trees, and tall well-kept hedges buffered the house from the street. Mr. Buster, when he wasn't working to earn money, always busied himself with a new home- or yard-improvement project.

Mr. Buster worked hard his whole life. He was a respected concrete mason and bricklayer, but when no call existed for these skills he picked cotton and peas, hauled hay, and dug post holes. He was one of the few black men in a mostly white town run by a white county sheriff and several bankers.

Mr. Buster, Lucy Belle, Mary, and I (I started at age eleven) picked a lot of peas. For our labor we were paid in kind, keeping half of what we picked. "Those peas," said Lucy Belle, "will stay in our freezer longer than money in our pockets."

Mabank is in black-eyed pea country. Not far down

the road in neighboring Athens, throngs converge every July for the Black-Eyed Pea Jamboree. Revelers enjoy square dancing, pea-shelling contests, pea-eating contests, and drinking a "pea-tini," a martini enhanced by a black-eyed pea instead of the customary olive. Curious, or perhaps courageous, connoisseurs can sample culinary concoctions made from original "reci-peas" for everything from bread to ice cream.

Lucy Belle Britt also worked hard, matching and surpassing her husband's 5:30 A.M.-to-dark schedule. She cleaned the mayor's barber shop (in the summer Mary and I relieved her of this job) and many of the white homes in Mabank. She stood five feet six inches, about the same height as Mr. Buster, and was governed by strong Baptist beliefs, although it hadn't always been that way—she'd had plenty of fun as a younger woman. She raised four children, including my mother, by herself (each had a different father, and she threw each man out in turn), before settling down with the reliable and industrious Mr. Buster. Even in her mid-fifties she was a strikingly handsome woman, and she looked everyone, white or black, straight in the eye.

My grandmother religiously took us to Sunday School and church every week. Choruses of "Amazing Grace," "How Great Thou Art," and "Rock of Ages" rose through the rafters. Heated hellfire-and-brimstone sermons often let out to dinner on the grounds, always a scrumptious feast prepared by some of the best cooks in the county.

Mabank, which sits near the east Texas pine country, featured rolling hills, idyllic green pastures, and a turn-of-the-century slow pace that didn't rush children into being adults.

I became a black Huck Finn, catching catfish, bass, and perch. I loved being alone on long, lazy, lovely Texas afternoons, daydreaming on the bank of the pond, knowing I'd have our dinner and more by day's end.

By the time I was ten I had hunted armadillos, rabbit, raccoon, and possum with a .22 rifle. I thought barbecued armadillo a gourmet delight, but when I grew up I could never persuade Too Tall Jones or any of my other Cowboy teammates to try it.

Even as very little children Mary and I had to work. "You're earning money for school clothes and such," Lucy Belle would say. In addition to picking cotton and black-eyed peas, we sold watermelon and helped our grandmother with her cleaning jobs.

The strong people in my life were all females: my mom, Lucy Belle, and even my sister, Mary. Mary once got so upset with me for not fighting a boy who taunted me that *she* went after him—and won, too.

Mary was my best friend during most of childhood, but our time together diminished as we grew. Mary was a beauty, gorgeous and stunning as a little girl, as a young woman, and now. She had movie star good looks and a personality as outgoing and gregarious as mine was introverted and isolated. She made friends naturally, both boys and girls, and always urged me to join them, but my shyness kept me away. I preferred being alone, reading, out at the pond with a fishing pole, or in my room in Dallas with my dreams.

We lived on the near north side of Dallas, close to downtown, and lying in my bed I could see from my window the Southland Life building, one of the city's first skyscrapers. I imagined myself being a respected and highly successful businessman going each day to my tastefully furnished offices on an upper floor of Southland Life. My other daydream involved starring for the Dallas Cowboys, who were then new in the city (1960 was the franchise's first year) but already capturing everyone's attention. Neither fantasy had much hope of coming true. I didn't even know what Southland Life did. And as for pro football, I was too awkward even to play with my peers. My skinny frame would be cut in half by one of those big NFL players.

One day in Dallas, in 1964, Philip Bluett, the neighborhood bully that year, took my baseball and wouldn't give it back. I ran inside our house and told my mother.

"Take it away from him," she said.

Philip was a bad-ass. I didn't make a move.

"Good Lord, Harvey," Mom said wearily, putting down the church bulletin she was reading. She marched me out on the front porch and surveyed the scene. About twenty kids stood around waiting to catch the show; and Philip Bluett, his feet wide apart, wearing an insolent smile and tossing my baseball from one hand to the other, held center stage.

"Go get the ball," said Mom.

"Give me the ball, Philip," I said.

"*Go get it, Harvey.*"

I asked for the ball again. Bluett didn't move. Well, I figured, he'd be in big trouble for defying my Mom.

"He won't give it to me," I said. I had six inches on the sturdy Bluett and didn't want to get whipped by him in front of twenty kids *plus* my mother. And whipped I would have been. The best maneuver my skinny frame could manage involved stumbling over my own feet.

It surprised me when Mom didn't go after Bluett. It surprised me even more when she whipped *me*, right in front of everybody. She produced the paddle with "bad stick" written on it and whaled away at my bony behind. The kids loved it. Bluett must have figured himself next in line because he gently tossed the baseball up on the porch and took off running.

I received a lot of whippings from my God-fearing mother: for lying about homework, failing to wash the dishes, forgetting to take out the trash. I learned what I was doing wrong.

We lived in the shadow of downtown Dallas, at 1819 Cudney Street. Today Woodall-Rogers Freeway runs high over where our house used to be. Our rented brown frame home had two bedrooms, a big kitchen, and a living room, and Mom maintained it immaculately. She'd bring out the bad stick whenever I left clothes on the floor or my bed unmade.

Obviously Mom—Helen—reigned as monarch in our house. She didn't allow Mary or me to argue with her, and still doesn't. If I washed dishes and left a smudge on just a single fork, *all* of them had to be done over. Missing a single patch of grass meant mowing the entire lawn again. Mom insisted Mary and I always do our best, and I know her lessons helped when later we were grown and had to survive among taskmasters just as demanding. We knew Mom loved us.

Mom worked as a cleaning lady and, like my grandmother, was much in demand. The homes she maintained as meticulously as our own were in Preston Hollow, a wealthy section of north Dallas. Often she managed the parties of the rich and afterward brought home some marvelous food. "Rich people throw good stuff away," she'd say disapprovingly.

Mom later sold encyclopedias—as determined as she was, I wonder how anyone ever turned her down—and was highly respected as the cashier at the Booker T. Washington High School cafeteria. I took plenty of beatings as a youngster (who'd pass up such an easy target?), but I remember Mom saved me from one and she wasn't even there. Two toughs—maybe they weren't, since everybody seemed tough to me—came up to me on the street and demanded my lunch money. One of them brandished a razor blade. "Hey, wait a minute," one said upon recognizing me. "That's Mrs. Martin the cashier's boy."

And just like that the two went searching for a different victim. It wasn't fear of my mother that prompted them to leave me alone, but respect.

My dad—Sylvester—drove a truck for the city of Dallas; quit to work for a furniture store, where he hurt his back lifting; and returned to the municipal job. Dad worked hard, had a reputation for reliability, and was a great handyman. We moved to a half-brick home on Haas Street in my eighth-grade year, and soon Dad had made it all-brick. The home was in the Oak Cliff section of Dallas, which many people considered the finest part of the city. We had three bedrooms and a big front and back yard. As fast as blacks, encouraged by open housing laws, moved into Oak Cliff, whites moved out, and today the area is primarily black.

Dad represented a solid, steady presence at home, but the room just didn't exist for him to wield the dominating influence on my life. When he thought to discipline, Mom had already done it. When he sought to advise, Mom had been there before him.

I remained a normal-sized kid until fifth grade. Then I just shot up, to six feet three inches in seventh grade, to almost six-six in high school. I would hit my head on a tree branch I'd previously walked under and think the tree had grown shorter. When I realized I'd gotten out of proportion to my environment, I began slouching a lot. I didn't want to stand out, to be tall. I found it merely made me a target. My innate shyness became more pronounced, made worse by my height, and increasingly I spent the bulk of my time alone.

In my sophomore year in high school, I got a job at Titche-Goettinger (Titche's) department store, earning $40.40 a week. Mom kept $20.20 of it. "I've been taking care of him all his life," she told a neighbor in a voice loud enough for me to hear. "Now Harvey can take care of me."

This always active woman didn't mean it, of course,

but her words made me puff up with importance and vow to myself to do a good job. I'm sure Mom had many things in her mind when she encouraged me to go to work, chiefly my interaction with people in a larger world.

So I scrubbed pots every day after school. I'd never been lazy, having kept up with men on a summer road crew and with Mr. Buster in the pea fields. With hustle and doing a good job, traits Mom had drilled into me, I advanced from pot washer to dish washer to busboy.

The Distributive Education Program at South Oak Cliff High let me out of school early to work forty hours a week at Titche's. And by never missing a day, never being late, volunteering to do more than required, I rose to what I considered the "top": The store put me on duty Saturdays, its biggest day, yet oddly at a time when most of the managers were off. I got up each Saturday at 5 A.M., took the bus downtown, and along with a single security guard prepared the place to open for business. I took early deliveries of goods, made certain the aisles sparkled, and later, when other employees arrived, directed the highly important traffic on dumbwaiters.

The job didn't hurt my grades. In seventh grade I'd had the highest marks of any boy in the class, and in high school usually made the honor roll. Mom's fanaticism about homework helped, but also, because of being introverted, I had plenty of time to study. I rarely engaged in normal social activities and didn't have a date until my senior year.

Mary tried harder than anyone to break me out of my shell of isolation. My good-looking, personable sister had friends enough for ten people and usually asked me to go out with them. "Come on, Harvey, you'll have fun."

I didn't think so. I dreaded the question so often asked me: "How can you be so ugly when you have such a pretty sister?"

I was indeed a sight. My bottom jaw was outgrowing

the top, and no one knew what to do about it. I looked almost freakish.

Sports Illustrated later called Mary "one of those children whom God kisses and gently blows from the womb," but she had a touch of the imp in her. I know one time she tattled to Mom and I got thrashed with the bad stick. The last of these spankings, incidentally, occurred when I was seventeen and at my present height of just a shade under six feet six inches.

We made quite a pair, the full-of-zip sister and the reclusive, bashful brother. I saw us as a sibling version of "Beauty and the Beast." Anyone with eyes could see beauty all over Mary. I loved her because she, like my mother and grandmother, looked with her heart and saw beauty in me.

Mary was a good athlete, a very fast runner. With proper coaching, extremely hard to find for a girl, she might have been an Olympic sprinter.

No one even thought *I* might possess sports skills. Certainly I didn't. In grammar school, just to get me out with other boys, Mom made me go out for a YMCA football team. On the very first play I literally got run over. It hurt some, seemed a terrible humiliation, but it must have appeared even worse to Mom, who'd come to watch. "My Lord, son," she said, "learn to play the piano. Or swim." Eventually I learned how to swim. But my first attempt to play football had ended in disaster.

In ninth grade Mary persuaded me to attend a pep assembly. Everybody jumped up and down, the band played, the kids yelled, and when the football players came in, well, the whole world could see that they were cool. They were somebodies. Girls reached out to touch their jackets, boys thumped them on the back. Here were these football players being showered with attention, almost adulation, and it had nothing to do with how they looked.

Playing football would make me cool, I reasoned. People wouldn't judge me by my jutting jaw, splayed teeth, or oversized legs and ears. Maybe some of my shyness, my fear of being around others, would disappear when students and even adults shook *my* hand and pounded *my* back. I showed up for football practice the next day and it was a disaster.

I couldn't forget what had happened to me with the YMCA team and found myself gripped by fear and cowardice. I believe the fear was more mental than physical. It had hurt, getting knocked over like a bowling pin, but I could endure pain if it helped break me out of my isolation, a much worse condition than bumps and bruises or even a broken bone. What caused me to fail was remembering the humiliation of that YMCA experience—my teammates laughing when I got flattened, *my mother watching*.

I knew I'd made a mistake even before I got out on the practice field. I'd fail, be humiliated again, confirm everyone's opinion of me as a nobody. Without inviting them I had enough problems, and here I'd foolishly gone looking for more.

It didn't help that I knew nothing about football. I didn't have the sketchiest notion of proper techniques, correct stances, or even what position I might play. Of course, you have to *learn* techniques, stances, and positions, and though I started late—for football-crazy Texas, at least—it obviously wasn't *too late*.

Except that I told myself it was. Everyone else on the field seemed to know what to do, and I magnified their skills in my mind. Each player had the ability of Johnny Unitas; the coach possessed the wisdom and know-how of Vince Lombardi.

What the coach *could* do was recognize a phony when he saw one. On the first day I exaggerated an eye injury to avoid a rough one-on-one drill, and when I persisted that I'd been hurt, he decided I shouldn't play in games. I did get my picture in the paper, though. Because my uniform was always clean, he had me pose at half-time with the homecoming queen.

In 1966, my sophomore year at J. N. Ervin High School, I worked like a demon at Titche's, glorying in small promotions, and achieved a degree of contentment whenever I squirreled up in my room. It didn't bother me that away from school and work I'd become a hermit. I thought my parents were proud of me, and I didn't have to endure the pain that always accompanied social contacts with my peers.

I went to South Oak Cliff High School (SOC) my eleventh grade year, and no one attending the school could be unaware of the great changes taking place. SOC, previously all white, had just become the first fully integrated major high school in Dallas. Blacks rushed to attend. Parents rightly believed it meant a better education for their children, and the kids themselves thought going there was the "in" thing to do.

SOC suddenly became a football powerhouse in a football-mad state. Burnis MacFarland may have made it happen. When this gifted running back announced that he intended to transfer from Lincoln High to SOC, many other top black athletes did the same. Six previously all-black schools contributed to the talent pool gathering at SOC, and overnight the Golden Bears became transformed into a dynamo, a legitimate contender for the coveted state championship.

High school football is a religion in Texas. Parents, coaches, and fans begin speculating on the potential of children when they're barely out of diapers. A common practice is to "red-shirt" *high school students*, that is, set up an extra year of eligibility for them. Only two sports exist in Texas, the saying goes—football and spring football.

I took considerable razzing at Titche's the summer before my junior year because I didn't plan to go out for football. I'd grown to my final height of nearly six feet six inches and weighed 220 pounds, but didn't realize the filling-out process meant most people wouldn't be running over me anymore. I figured I could endure the razzing at work.

But I overheard Dad say something I *couldn't* endure. He'd just returned from the golf course, and didn't know I was listening. "All the guys at the club are bragging about their boys being on the football team," he told Mom. "I can never brag about my boy."

I'd thought he was proud of me. Now I felt empty and sick to my stomach. I retreated to my room in confusion. I'd even failed Mom and Dad and Mary, the people who counted most to me. I slumped on the bed, tears forming in my eyes, wanting to kick myself, pummel myself, bang my head against the wall. I really was a nothing, a wretched nobody, and bore no resemblance whatever to the dashing football player of my fantasy.

When the despair lessened, I made up my mind to do two things: I'd go out for football, and I wouldn't quit. I'd surely get cut from the team, a mixed blessing, but at least I'd try.

The next day, after I managed to have my hours at Titche's rearranged, Mom and Mary drove me to the football field. I was two weeks late and the last player to go out for the team. Had someone been asked to choose from this glittering display of high school athletic talent the player who'd make the biggest name for himself in the sport, I'd have been the very last selection.

No decent equipment remained when I showed up for practice. "What size shoe do you wear?" a student manager asked.

"Twelve."

"This is all we've got."

It was an eleven. I squeezed the shoes on and the pain started. I didn't know if I could walk in them, much less run. Next I received a helmet with the strap missing and an uncovered screw on the inside that bored a hole into my head whenever I made the slightest contact. Because of my size I got assigned to the defensive line, under Assistant Coach Norman Jett, a truly remarkable man destined to reach near-legendary status at South Oak Cliff.

It rained that first day. Luckily, I didn't hear Coach Jett pronounce his first judgment of me: "He looks like a dying calf in a thunderstorm."

If I'd hoped to be cut from the team, I soon learned it wouldn't happen. Because of the touchy issue of integration, school administrators had ruled that *no* black would be cut from the football team. I suspect they feared lawsuits.

I still didn't know the first thing about football. I

thought perhaps my shoes were *supposed* to be too small, that it was a method used to toughen up players. Perhaps the same held true for the missing helmet strap and the screw boring into my head. But the worst was my not possessing even rudimentary techniques. I thrashed about like a fish out of water.

Norman Jett stood six feet four inches and weighed 260 pounds, and he was a tough coach even by Texas standards. He loved putting us against the seven-man sled and having us bang it, an excellent way to teach kids to stay low and deliver a maximum-impact blow. Jett became enraged at anything less than maximum effort; he'd actually foam at the mouth, spewing saliva in every direction as he shouted. Occasionally he got so mad he'd pick up a player and throw him against the sled.

Coach Jett yelled at me as much as anyone, maybe more, but he spent extra time with me, too. My many weaknesses were not the result of failing to try—after overhearing what Dad said, I'd promised myself to do my best—but of an adolescent awkwardness I hadn't completely outgrown. It hurt that I hadn't participated in sports when I'd been younger. (Hopscotch with Mary—not to be sneered at because it develops agility—was just about the extent of my athletic endeavors.) And it hurt, too, that I had to learn football fundamentals my teammates long since had absorbed as second nature.

But my biggest handicap was my lack of any aggressiveness. Shying away from trouble had become an ingrained habit. I'd never started a fight, much less ever assaulted anybody. I didn't even raise my voice. To be a good defensive lineman, a player has got to be mean. Sportswriters say "Mean Joe" Greene acquired his nickname because of his college, North Texas State, "the Mean Green," but I know the "mean" stuck because of how he played.

Coach Jett patiently explained what I'd have to do to

make myself tough. It didn't have to be part of your birthright—probably wasn't. You became that way—but only on the football field—because that's what the game required.

Coach Jett also spent time teaching me the fundamentals, a job he couldn't have enjoyed. He possessed an excellent football mind—it would have translated into a Ph.D. in tactics and strategy if such a degree were awarded. He told me I had potential, and this recognition steeled me to endure almost anything—tough practices under a boiling sun, Jett's screaming, a body so beat up I had to get out of bed sideways in the morning, and very little measurable progress.

I did get the equipment problem ironed out. About two weeks into practice, after a session with the seven-man sled, blood streaked down my forehead onto my face. "Let me see your helmet, son," Coach Jett said.

I showed it to him.

"Well, this isn't good," he understated. "We'll get you a new one."

I asked if my shoes were supposed to be too small, and he obtained a proper size. I blew these two minor triumphs out of all proportion, reasoning that I must indeed show potential if this important man concerned himself with my comfort. I worked harder than ever to improve. I still have a small recognizable scar on my forehead where the screw in that first helmet gouged its hole.

South Oak Cliff went 9–1 my junior year, our only defeat being a 7–6 loss to Sunset in an early game, before we realized how good we were. I played only in blowouts, of which there were several, but did get into more games than Coach Jett later remembered. After I'd been named All-Pro, when asked about my junior year in high school, this man who gave me so much help said, "We beat one team 77–7. Harvey *might* have got in that game."

I continued working at Titche's, taking care not to lose

my Saturday morning slot. We played football games on Friday nights, so getting up the next day at 5 A.M. posed a test of sorts, one I always managed to pass.

One day during spring training before my senior year, Jett told me to fill in for a tired defensive lineman during a scrimmage. I actually managed to make a couple of hard tackles. "That's the way to go!" Jett yelled, making me feel ten feet tall. I yearned for praise. I figured if making tackles would earn it, well, I'd make a lot of tackles.

The coaches hadn't known where to play me until this scrimmage. I was big, so naturally they put me in the line, but should I be on offense or defense? After that scrimmage, I never played another down of offense.

The biggest difference for me between offense and defense is hitting or getting hit. On defense you hit. On offense you get hit. Some of the best offensive linemen seem to be sponges, soaking up punishment, fearsome blows that rearrange the brain, but they're effective because you can't get around them. At least figuratively, I'd been the hittee often enough. I wanted to be the *hitter*.

By the end of spring practice I'd matured considerably, more physically than mentally, but improvements were evident in both areas. Technically I still had a whole world to master. Lining up in the wrong stance, being off balance, not knowing *how* to hit or be hit, all cause a player to mess up. They can also get him hurt.

I'll never forget the last words Coach Jett said to me that spring: "Harvey, if you're riding the bench this season, you'll be the biggest kid in Dallas who's not playing, and I'll be the laughingstock of the coaches' association for not shaping you up."

I worked out hard all summer. To improve my agility I spent an hour each day on a drill Coach Jett recommended. I'd place a long, two-foot wide board on the ground, straddle the board, and charge forward, as fast as I could go, trying never to touch the wood. When fall practice began, I did this better than anyone on the team.

Echoes of Coach Jett's yell, "That's the way to go, Harvey!" kept me pushing harder, and when the season opened I found myself in the starting lineup at defensive end.

In addition to my size I had speed, something I had never known I possessed. In fact, I've been timed at 4.65 seconds for 40 yards, a speed not many quarterbacks can match. Besides being able to hit hard, I could run people down from behind.

In my junior year SOC had sixty blacks and twenty whites on the team, but the next season only four whites remained. All were good, tough players—starters and good guys. Too bad others didn't stay around, because they would have been part of one fine football team.

SOC's 1968 football squad didn't beat teams; we trampled them. We defeated North Dallas High 62–0, and Booker T. Washington 68–0. College scouts came from all over the country to watch us play. Running back Hodge Mitchell seemed the reincarnation of the great Jim Brown, a power back with the breakaway potential to go all the way on every play. Hodge received a scholarship to play at Florida State.

Charlie Slaughter, our nose guard, was another who went on to bigger things in college. And Danny Colbert went even farther: He played for the San Diego Chargers. Colbert was a vicious hitter; so was linebacker Tommy Powell—big, fast, and agile, a state wrestling champ *and* Golden Gloves champ. Our quarterback was a white stud named Mike McDaniel who could throw the ball long or short to a bevy of speedy receivers. Mike later played for North Texas State.

Every starter on our team, except me, made one or other of the All-District teams that coaches and reporters select at the end of the year. It was enough for me just to be part of the SOC lineup. The team spirit was wonderful, and so was the school's. Best of all, people didn't make fun of my looks or my shyness anymore. I belonged to a team that folks from UCLA, Notre Dame, and Oklahoma came to see. It didn't matter that they didn't seem to notice me. Mom, Dad, and Mary never missed a game.

We breezed to a 10–0 record in 1968 and met a tough Bryan Adams team for the city championship. Some 19,000 fans packed Cobb Stadium that Friday night. I remember on the way to the game being caught on the team bus in a four-mile-long traffic jam, and being amazed to find out the backup was caused by our game.

All city championship games in Dallas were an event, but this one was something else, something people haven't forgotten—maybe for the wrong reason. Bryan Adams had an all-white team; we had just those four white starters. There was plenty of talk, some of it ugly, all of it emanating from adults. The two teams just wanted to get it on, go all-out, and see who was best.

The teams might not have been models of integration, but our side of the stands had an equal mixture of white and black. I couldn't find a black face on the Bryan Adams side.

The son of my boss at Titche's played for Bryan Adams. I'd taken plenty of kidding at work about what BA would do to us. I didn't think so. I didn't think they could stop Hodge Mitchell or Burnis MacFarland, or that they'd get anywhere against a defense anchored by Charlie Slaughter, Danny Colbert, and Tommy Powell—and me. I'd improved tremendously. Coach Jett later said that I was the best player on the team at this time. I didn't make those All-District teams because I didn't start the season fast and get noticed immediately. Later, when I blossomed, the writers were already watching other people.

But I had indeed learned to play football; and I possessed size, speed, and quickness. I wasn't textbook perfect, like Jethro Pugh, but in high school I didn't have to be.

Image looms important to high school kids. I didn't just want to beat Bryan Adams; I wanted our entire school to look good doing it. Bryan Adams took the field first. The players came out on the field through rows of cheerleaders, their fans screaming, their band blaring a victory march. It looked big-time, like something you'd see at the Orange Bowl, and it had to puff up the Bryan Adams players. Well, we'd go out like we always did, I thought. We might lose in the image department, but we'd win the game.

I underestimated my own classmates. On the spur of the moment, the band and pep squad (my sister, Mary, among them) and cheerleaders lined up in two columns, a human aisle, for our grand entry onto the field. I don't think any of us had ever felt so important. I thought, even doing it impromptu, our fans had outshone their opposition.

Thinking about image, if only for a moment, was a mistake for our players. We had a different job to do, and almost failed. Reporter Mike Jones, writing for the *Dallas Morning News,* described what happened:

A sophomore field goal kicker, Vernon Denwitty, dramatically put the foot back in football as he kicked a 29-yard field goal with 1:47 left in the game, and South Oak Cliff escaped with its life and a bi-district championship, 13–12, over determined Bryan Adams before 19,000 fans at Cobb Stadium Friday night. . . .

Boasting four of the quickest backs in the state, the Bears for some reason known only to the Ghost of Christmas Past deserted their sparkling ground game for a passing attack which resulted in two interceptions; and it could have been worse.

It took another fantastic charge by the SOC defense and a 26-yard punt return by halfback Hodge Mitchell to pull it out of the fire and set the stage for Denwitty's decisive boot.

I had one of my best games against Bryan Adams. Caught up in the excitement of our undefeated season, I scarcely noticed how much easier things came to me. I didn't have to think before putting one foot in front of the

other, as I'd had to before. Doing the right thing began to
come naturally, the result of practice, repetition, and the
normal maturing process.

The following week, when we were 40 or so points
ahead against Arlington Heights in the state tournament,
an unfortunate event occurred. One of the Arlington players, no doubt frustrated and angry at the ignominious end
to his season, seemed to deliberately clip our star running
back, Hodge Mitchell, leaving Hodge writhing on the
ground in agony with a leg injury.

Our last game was both my best and worst. We took
our 12–0 record up against Houston Smylie at Texas A&M
Stadium and got beat 7–0. Hodge Mitchell appeared for
one play, a 15-yard gain, and reinjured his leg. Our defense sparkled the entire night, but the offense couldn't
move the ball.

It was my best game because I'd become a genuine
force on defense, a player with power, speed, and determination. It was my worst because we'd lost and would
not become state champions, as we'd all dreamed. Each
of us had suffered our first important athletic defeat, and I
didn't think the tears in the locker room, and later on the
bus, and later still at home in our rooms, would ever stop.
For me, of course, there would be more heartbreaking
defeats up the road, infinitely larger than this one, but
many more ups than downs, wins than losses. In my
despair I never imagined a future in football. I believed I'd
played my last game.

But not if Coach Norman Jett had his way. Recruiters
flocked to South Oak Cliff. Although they didn't come to
see me, Coach Jett made sure they heard my name. He'd
sit them down and show them the game films against
Houston Smylie. He also called all over the country for
me, telling everyone he could get on the phone about "this
kid with great potential who's willing to learn."

No one in my family had attended college. I didn't
think I'd be the first. My plans went no further than

working for Titche's (I'd kept the job all through high school) and seeing how far I could rise there. I thanked Coach Jett often for his efforts but couldn't imagine him succeeding. Besides, doubts set in: My progress on the football field began to seem like a dream. Maybe I'd just been lucky in high school. Against the "big boys" in college I'd probably be brought down hard.

Eventually the persistent Norman Jett began to obtain results. I received letters from Oklahoma, Nebraska, New Mexico, and Penn State. But the first coach to show up at our house was a small bundle of energy named Boley Crawford from East Texas State University.

The whole family was waiting for him. I'd insisted on our making a good impression. When Dad let him into the house I jumped to my feet, walked toward him, a big smile on my face, hand outstretched.

He went right by me to my mother, who was sitting at the dining room table. "I'm Boley Crawford," he said. "So nice to meet you, Mrs. Martin."

Mom took his hand. I could tell she was pleased. "Well, it's nice to meet *you*, Mr. Crawford."

I stood foolishly, the smile frozen on my face, my hand still extended. Much later I heard the famous basketball coach Al McGuire say that he always tried to recruit the mother, not the athlete. I had witnessed this philosophy at work. Certainly, Boley Crawford paid no attention to me.

"This surely is a lovely home, Mrs. Martin."

"Well, thank you, Mr. Crawford."

"I understand you work, Mrs. Martin. How do you find the time to do all this?"

"Oh, Harvey and Mary help around the house. I'm sorry, Mr. Crawford—this is my daughter, Mary. Mary, say hello to Mr. Crawford."

"You're a beautiful young lady, Mary."

Blushing. "Thank you."

"What kind of work do you do, Mrs. Martin?"

"This and that. One thing is I sell encyclopedias."

"You do?"

"Yes."

"What a coincidence! My own son has been wanting a set of encyclopedias. Could you show me yours?"

Of course, he bought a set. He still hadn't said a word to me. I stood behind Mom and wondered if he ever would.

He did, but only at the end of his interview with my mother, as he left the house. Before that, for more than an hour, he and Mom talked about everything under the sun—from how to cook black-eyed peas to religion. Boley Crawford enchanted my mom, but I think it worked the other way, too.

Finally he broached what I considered the point. "East Texas State is a fine school, Mrs. Martin."

"I'm sure it is, Mr. Crawford."

"We hope Harvey will attend on one of our fine athletic scholarships."

"That's up to him. I'm sure you understand."

Really? I still wonder how seriously Boley Crawford took this remark.

"Our school isn't far away. Harvey will be close to home."

The man was uncanny. He seemed to know exactly what to say, exactly what a mother wanted to hear.

"I promise you, Mrs. Martin, we'll feed your boy all he can eat."

Mary snickered and I wanted to smack her.

"Harvey will need wholesome food," Mom said.

"And he'll get it. You have my promise, Mrs. Martin."

Outside on the lawn Coach Crawford finally spoke to me. "Harvey," he said, "we know you don't know much about football. Come to East Texas State and grow up with us."

Mom talked constantly in the days that followed about what a "nice man" Boley Crawford was, at the same time steadfastly assuring me the decision rested with me. But I knew where she wanted me to go. She worried that I wasn't ready for life away from home, and "nice" Mr. Crawford, with a son who wanted encyclopedias, would keep a protective, fatherly eye on me.

Chad Brown, a six foot six, 280-pound senior at East Texas State, about to be drafted by the Pittsburgh Steelers, drove me to Commerce, Texas, and showed me around the school. I didn't think Chad lied to me when he said I'd like East Texas State. This big, intelligent All-American lineman stated the facts quietly, with no sell at all.

And I bought. I bought because of Chad . . . and especially because of Boley Crawford. Coach Crawford hadn't lied to me. He'd told me straight out that I didn't know much, that I had a lot to learn. I knew it was true. When other recruiters, from much more prestigious schools, assured me I'd be starting as a freshman and make All-American "your second year, third year at the latest," I knew it *wasn't* true.

Nonsense. I'd been a regular in high school just one year, a decent player for only a few games. With Mom's full-hearted concurrence, I decided "to come to East Texas State and grow up" with them.

Nobody promised me I'd start as a freshman, but I did. Attitude had a lot to do with it. Since football had gotten me into college, where I very much wanted to be, I was determined to be serious about the game. My play even during practice could best be characterized as gung-ho—all out—and sometimes teammates didn't appreciate it. Why hit a friend hard? Why not save the physical stuff for an opponent?

I figured if you didn't tackle hard in practice, you might not be able to in a game. More important, scholarships didn't come with a guarantee at East Texas State. I had to impress the coaches, or I might find myself back at Titche's, coordinating dumbwaiters.

At East Texas State I lived at Stone Hall and shared small quarters with three roommates: Dwight White, soon to be part of the Pittsburgh Steelers' famed Steel Curtain; Arthur "Sugar Bear" McClaren from New Jersey; and my friend Burnis MacFarland from South Oak Cliff. None of us questioned that Dwight White, known as Mad Dog, six feet five inches and 260 mean pounds, had the final say in any arguments that arose.

Dwight was the first person I met at East Texas State. I lugged in a trunk and set it down in the room, and there he sat, filling a chair to overflowing, a big bear ready to bite someone's head off.

"Hey, kid," he growled in what I learned served as his normal voice, "get yourself next door. It's shavin' time."

"Shavin' time?"

"You're gonna get your hair cut off."

"Why?"

"Because you're a freshman. Now get going!"

"I don't want my head shaved."

"I like you, boy. Damned if I know why, but I like you. Now do yourself a favor and move yourself over there."

"Awww . . ."

"It's for your own good."

And it was. Freshman football players had their heads shaved—or maybe cut in a checkerboard pattern or in a heart with an arrow through it. It was a tradition. And woe to the rookie who objected. He'd probably been a high school hotshot with big local headlines, and seniors would look to make life miserable for him on the field. If a running back, he might suddenly find himself without blockers. If a lineman, he could receive double- and triple-team attention.

I believe the head-shaving served a positive purpose. It told a newcomer, no matter how flashy his press clippings, that he belonged to a *team*. The *team* believed in head-shaving, and he damn well could suppress his ego. Sacrifice. Do what *others* wanted.

Dwight White soon became the big brother I'd never had. A junior when I arrived, he knew all the ropes, had all the right moves. On the field he tended to business, working like a Trojan to achieve a single-minded goal: being drafted by an NFL team.

It helped that he was naturally vicious—not off the field, where he could be as civilized as the next guy, but out between the striped lines. He was simply relentless—never stopped pounding on an opponent. Dwight didn't cry when he took a hit. In the first game of my freshman year he came out of play with a loose front tooth. I watched him reach in his mouth, pull the tooth out, then go right back on the field.

Everything Dwight did seemed cool to me. I couldn't get enough of his ideas on football, on life, on life after football. He intended to be a businessman when he hung up the cleats, he said, and sure enough he was. Dwight drove a Volkswagen in college, his knees up to his neck in the tiny car, and somehow I fitted inside with him.

Dwight impressed me enormously, but it didn't work the other way. Recalling our times together in college, he told a *Sports Illustrated* reporter: "Harvey was a thousand percent different than now. He was a big Baby Huey. He was so gentle, small guys used him as an ego-builder. Take his name, even—Harvey is not exactly a thundering name. Guys would push him around, and he felt so bad about himself it was easy to embarrass him. Everybody borrowed money off him. He was more or less a chump."

I may have been pushed around off the field—I did have trouble saying no to people—but not on. I became physically sure of myself before I developed mental confidence. Also, I didn't do much socializing. The shyness of my childhood didn't shed easily. I studied and worked at part-time jobs in college while others had dates and nights on the town. I envied them. Still, I'd traveled quite a distance from the years I spent holed up alone in my room.

East Texas had a *Wunderkind* running back named Arthur James, who could do it all. We called him King Arthur. His offensive linemen wore lettering across their backsides that boasted, "I BLOCK FOR THE KING." Dwight sported "I TACKLE THE KING" across his rear. Royalty didn't impress him.

King Arthur James was something special, by any measurement. He had speed, power, and grace. All the coaches pegged him a Number One draft pick, a pro star. But Arthur never made it. He got invited to participate in a post-season All-Star game and became enraged when he was excluded from a party all the white All-Stars attended. To protest, he boycotted the game. The "black power" salutes at the 1968 Mexico City Olympics were still fresh in everyone's mind. Arthur James never made it in the NFL.

Sugar Bear McClaren didn't feel he needed to attend an All-Star game to experience prejudice. This New Jerseyan believed the school was packed with racists, but I never saw them. Life seemed no different from what it had been in Dallas. The school may indeed have been racist, as Sugar Bear constantly told me, but I had no gauge against which to measure. McClaren ultimately quit the team.

At first the coaches conducted two-a-day practices. Compared to these muscle-achers, our high school drills had been a romp on the playground. After the morning session, we ate lunch. Then total exhaustion necessitated a nap to recharge our batteries before going back to the field at 3 P.M. for more torture under a hot Texas sun until 6. We hurt through dinner and later passed out on our beds. The worst part dawned the next morning when we dragged our bodies out of the sack to do it all over again.

We had quite a collection of coaches. There was Boley Crawford, of course, who worked with the offense and also tutored the golf team. Through him I picked up spending money caddying at the golf course.

Boley, if anything, was animated. "You're pitiful!" he'd yell at Luther Johnson, an offensive lineman. "You make me sick!"

Players who didn't live up to his expectations, he called "drut," which is *turd* spelled backward, and each one came to know if he deserved being called drut. The last practice of the day involved kickoffs from which the regulars were excused. "All druts on the field!" Boley would scream. As if by magic, the right players—or wrong—always knew who Boley meant.

Head Coach Ernest Hawkins knew a lot about football and gained a reputation as a quarterback-maker, developing such future pro quarterbacks as Wade Wilson, Will Cureton, and Jim Dietz. No one messed with Hawkins; he could take your scholarship away, and there was no appeal.

But the assistant coaches stand out in my memory most. Ron West, my defensive coach, appeared insane to me. "Go! Go! Go!" he'd yell. "Move! Move! Move!" he'd bellow. "You're a hitter! You're a hitter! You're a hitter!" he'd scream, even if the player pounded with the power of a powder puff. Ron West never shut up. He'd tried out for the pros once, which made him *the man*. "You've got ability, Harvey. Ability! Ability! Ability!" Then he'd yell again, sometimes into the sky, "Go! Go! Go! Move! Move! Move!" West spoke in threes.

Stumblin' Sam McCord, former All-American at East Texas State, was another persistent coach. Stumblin' Sam got his name from his playing days, when he'd stagger forward like a sailor on leave from his ship, somehow always keeping his feet, no matter how often he got hit.

Then there was Russell Ceratta, who had granite features and a build like Hercules. He was a supertough taskmaster who worked us like dogs.

East Texas State played in the Lone Star Conference, called the "best small conference in the United States." At that time the football-prestigious Southwest Conference (University of Texas, SMU, TCU, Texas A&M, Baylor, and others) didn't want many blacks, so most of us went to the Lone Star Conference.

SMU told me, "You don't have enough math."

Sure. Look at how many times SMU has been on NCAA probation. If I'd been white, I'd have had enough math.

Hodge Mitchell, Danny Colbert, and Raymond Rhodes were among the first blacks at TCU, but none of them stayed.

East Texas State played schools like Sul Ross, which is in Alpine, Texas, near El Paso, a two-day bus trip from Commerce. Sul Ross always had tough players. It's the only school I know where you can take courses in rodeo.

Besides caddying, I found work with Fidelity Union Life Insurance Company. I must have buttonholed every student on the East Texas State campus, persuading them to talk to a company salesman about insurance needs. I got paid $10 apiece for the first three students who agreed to an appointment, $20 for the second three, and $40 for every one after that. I made $260 in a single week, which made me the richest player on the team. I always had money in my pockets, which I readily lent to friends, as Dwight White pointed out. After I talked to everyone at East Texas State, I went to other campuses and canvassed. I had enormous energy and always used it.

I drank only once in college. After a game with Southwest Louisiana State in Lafayette, Louisiana, Dwight White, Jim Dietz, and I went with a considerable contingent of white and black football players to a bar called The Keg. The blacks didn't know it, but we were the first of our race to be served there. At Dwight's encouragement I drank forty cups of beer, which put me in a very happy mood.

"Somebody called me a nigger," Dwight hissed at me from across the table.

"Nah," I said.

"Somebody called me a nigger!" Dwight growled, pounding his fist on the table, standing up, getting ready to fight the entire bar. One of the players, maybe Dietz, calmed him down. Dwight could have caused some major damage.

I threw up all the way home on the bus, and didn't

drink again until I left college for the pros. Other players were less abstemious.

I played defensive tackle at ETSU and Dwight played defensive end, positions that would be reversed in the NFL. Before Dwight left for the Steelers at the end of my sophomore year, he flashed ten $100 bills in my face—his bonus money from the Steelers, the most money I'd ever seen. I said to myself, "Hey, Harvey, you got to work hard and get some of that."

"There will never be another Mad Dog," Dwight told me when he left for glory with the Steelers.

Yeah, I thought. *But I'll be better than you.*

Before the start of my senior year, I bet Boley Crawford a steak dinner that I'd make All-America. I've enjoyed very few meals as much as the one he bought at the Texas Steak House across from the campus; I ate steak and he ate crow.

Scholastically I did what I had to do to pass. One semester I actually made the Dean's List. Athletically I did more than I had to.

My sister, Mary, and my parents came to every game they could. Mary, who attended Mountain View Junior College, was the most popular girl in school, and it filled me with pride that she'd give up a weekend night to see her brother play.

East Texas State defeated Carson Newman for the NAIA National Championship, and I received letters from every NFL team. I dutifully filled out all the forms. Each asked where I wanted to play. My answer: "Anywhere."

I didn't hear from anywhere, but rumors swirled that I'd be drafted in an early round.

The day of the draft found me a near basket case. I tooled around Commerce in my car, alone, listening to radio station KVIL, which announced the draft choices as they came in. I heard, "B. J. DuPree, Cowboys, first round." I continued to drive. Next I heard, "Golden Richards, Cowboys, second round." Then I heard,

"Banks Martin, Cowboys, third round." Discouraged, I drove to the dorm. Gil Brandt of the Cowboys was on the phone.

"Harvey?"

"Yes."

"We just drafted you in the third round."

I was Banks Martin!

"You sure?"

"You're our property. When you can, come around to see us."

So I really was a Cowboy. My childhood dream had come true. If I didn't make the team, I vowed, it wouldn't be because anybody outworked me.

4

My grandmother, Lucy Belle Britt, died the week before the Cowboys drafted me. I felt I'd lost a mother, for indeed I'd actually had two mothers. I know how proud she would have been of her grandson.

My draft by the Cowboys put Dad in a quandary. He belonged to that tiny, but hardy band of Dallasites who hate the home team and always bet against them. "Well," I told him, "you'll just have to change."

I used Abner Haynes as my agent. A former AFL great with the Kansas City Chiefs, Abner had formed SCORE, a business designed to serve all an athlete's needs. Abner, a great talker, represented Dwight White, Rayfield Wright, Mean Joe Greene, Jethro Pugh, and Duane Thomas. Right away Abner had me invest in a nightclub named Balls, on Lemon Avenue. It featured—what else?—a pair of balls as its sign out front, though these wisely got removed before the place opened.

I loved being at Abner's office. I spent all my time there.

Abner took me over to the Cowboys office. Hot ripples of excitement trembled inside me, but I tried to stay cool and steady as I firmly shook hands with Gil Brandt. When defensive back Cornell Green walked in, I thought I'd faint. I'd seen him play so often on TV; he was like a god

32

to me. But face to face I was surprised that he had real flesh and bone—a normal person.

Then offensive tackle Rayfield Wright walked in and he was a god, the absolute best in the world at his position. As I stood up to shake hands, my heart sank. Rayfield, at six feet seven inches and 275 pounds, appeared twice as big as me. I knew he would be blocking me in practice, and I wondered how on earth I could ever make an impression on the coaches if I had to get around this giant.

Incredibly—was his coach mad?—Rayfield played free safety and tight end in college. This dynamo was quick, agile, huge, and mean, a breed of offensive lineman who didn't believe in the passive role. Other offensive linemen used to sit back and absorb blows, like human sponges, willing to soak up any form of physical abuse to keep the defensive player off the back of the quarterback. Not Rayfield. He'd *attack* his defensive opponent and try to destroy him.

That day in Abner's office I could feel Rayfield sizing me up with the monumental disdain every All-Pro has for a rookie.

I received a $20,000 salary my first year, plus an $18,000 bonus and a new Grand Prix. I sold the car back to the Cowboys for $7,500. Abner wanted me to buy a Riviera, but first I called my Number One advisor about getting a Cadillac Eldorado. "You've always wanted that car, Harvey," Mom said. "This might be the only chance you'll ever have to own it."

"Suppose you don't make the team?" asked Cadillac dealer Rodger Meier, later a friend.

"I'm not worried about making the team," I said with the brashness and ignorance of youth. "I'm worried about playing."

Did these words come out of the mouth of the same guy who had just felt dwarfed standing next to Rayfield Wright?

I took the Eldorado back to ETS during my final semester and became a BMOC, Big Man on Campus. I loved the attention but never forgot what I needed to do. I worked out harder on my own than the ETS coaches had ever worked me in those two-a-days. I didn't know what I'd do if I didn't make the Cowboys. I *had* to make the Cowboys.

Being represented by Abner Haynes provided me with one big advantage over other rookies. Before I ever practiced with the Cowboys, Abner had me work out with Dwight White and Mean Joe Greene, two of his other clients, in Grand Prairie, Texas, near Dallas. It was eye-opening to see how these established, already great players drove themselves. What I considered tough at ETS now seemed a stroll in the park compared to Grand Prairie. I thought if Mean Joe and Mad Dog had to kill themselves like this, I, the rookie, would have to beat my head into the ground just to stay alive.

Many rookies, with no conception of what they're getting into when they join an NFL team, are out virtually before they ever start. The difference between college and the NFL is night and day. Coaches in the NFL don't fool with you. You come in ready to play the first day, or you're gone—unless, of course, you're a Tony Dorsett, which I wasn't. You don't work yourself into shape at rookie training camp; you're either in shape or you're out of a job. Practicing with Dwight White and Joe Greene gave me an edge over other rookies who hoped they could ride their college press clippings right onto the team.

I reported for rookie training camp in March 1973. The Cowboys put us up at the Hilton Inn in Dallas.

"I'm Drew," said the first rookie I met, Drew Pearson, my roommate, who would become my lifelong friend. Drew was a free agent, which meant the odds were high against his lasting more than a few days. But he not only made it, he became one of the Cowboy greats.

"I'm Harvey," I said.

I was the fifty-third player chosen in the overall NFL draft and third for the Cowboys. When reporters asked Coach Tom Landry why I didn't go higher, he said, "Harvey's from a small school. The competition wasn't that tough."

This made me feel terrible. But Tex Schramm, president and general manager of the Cowboys, had encouraging words: "Harvey's the kind of player who can help us for ten years."

I did it for eleven.

A bus took us to the practice field at Forest Lane and Abrams Road. I noticed that players from big, prestigious schools had their chests out. Those like myself, from little schools, looked dejected. The coaches had us jog, sprint, run a mile, lift weights. This part wasn't too tough. The relatively light workout, actually a warm-up exercise, gave some players the impression it would be a breeze. Thanks to Dwight and Mean Joe, I knew better.

In April I came from ETS and joined other rookies to attend veteran camp. The griping I heard struck me the most. Everybody had a complaint: The water in the showers was either too hot or too cold; the disinfectant was too strong or it wasn't strong enough. And why the hell did veterans have to be working out in April anyway? Again, unless a rookie had the advance knowledge I had, he obtained no idea what he was going up against.

I tried to keep my mind on business, yet I couldn't help but gawk. There I was, standing next to television heroes Roger Staubach, Craig Morton, Mel Renfro, Bob Lilly, Jethro Pugh. Many of them were already Super Bowl champions, and I was just a snot-nosed kid out of a jerkwater east Texas college.

I wasn't so awed that I forgot how to count. I counted defensive linemen. The Cowboys had Bob Lilly, Jethro Pugh, Larry Cole, Pat Toomay, and Bill Gregory, which added up to five; and I figured they'd need six. This meant if I didn't let some eager beaver sneak up on me, if I worked harder than I had ever dreamed possible, I'd be number six. The Cowboys had traded Tody Smith, Bubba's brother, to Houston after he got in a spat with offensive line coach Jim Myers. Myers said something Tody didn't like, and Tody chased him around the field "to kill him." It was sort of okay to differ with an assistant coach, but never to fight with him, and you weren't even supposed to breathe in front of a head coach. With a head coach, and especially Landry, you just listened and said, "Yessir."

Defensive line coach Ernie Stautner, a Hall-of-Famer who'd played with the Steelers, didn't particularly mind that Tody chased Myers. Stautner didn't like the offense; Coach Myers didn't like the defense.

It wasn't long before I figured Stautner didn't like me. He yelled at me all the time, and it took years before he stopped. I guess he thought I needed screaming at. I figured I was a self-starter, not someone who needed to be yelled at.

The griping among the veterans continued to amaze me. The great Bob Lilly never wanted to run. The practices were too long for Pat Toomay. Nobody liked the food. Coach Landry heard all this—nobody hid the complaining from him. All the veteran players called him "Tom." A rookie wouldn't dare. Veterans had built this team and figured they had the right to call Landry by his first name.

Situated in front of the coaches' table in the dining hall was the Fat Man's Table, bearing a caricature of a beer-bellied player with flies circling his head and his finger in his mouth. Willie Townes was a regular at the Fat Man's Table. He ate only soup at meals and still remained overweight. After meals, out of the coaches' sight, Willie would gobble something like eight bologna sandwiches and drink a six-pack of beer in his room.

I was the last player ever to sit at the Fat Man's Table. Ernie Stautner thought my 265 pounds should trim down to 252. I viewed my place at the table as another example of Ernie singling me out.

I was a sprinter, but the Cowboys kept making me run distances. I hated long runs, but worst of all, I didn't get the chance to impress with my main asset, my speed. Over a distance, I was the slowest player on the team.

Once in rookie camp I faked an ankle injury. "I stepped in a hole," I told Stautner.

"Keep running," he said. And I had to do an *extra* three-quarters of a mile lap.

Alvin Roy, the Cowboy weight coach, an old guy and one of the first to recognize the importance of lifting weights, became a favorite of mine. "Do those squats," he'd say, "and you'll get that little girl and wear her out."

"Harvey," Roy told me, "I visited my girl friend's daddy's grave yesterday. I learned I was born *before* him. You know why I outlived him? Squats."

Roy thought of us as "his boys," and he always had time for rookies. When Too Tall Jones joined the team the next year, 1974, Alvin Roy took him home and worked with him.

Alvin left the team a few years after I arrived, and things got more sophisticated. Stuff like karate, stretching, ballet, and aerobics were introduced. Those are cute, but I never thought much of them. You've got to move guys—hit them. Alvin, Too Tall, and I were from the old school.

I lived at home. Three days before going to the Cowboys' official training camp at Thousand Oaks, California, I told Mom I was going to run a distance. I decided on two miles. Ernie Stautner wanted me to run distances, so by God I'd do it. I'd do anything he suggested to help me make the team. I drove to a stretch of ground along the LBJ Freeway, found a stop sign, clocked my car another mile, and parked it. This was July, a blistering hot Texas afternoon, but I took off back to that stop sign, feeling good. I left the car motor running with the air conditioner on so I'd have something to look forward to when I returned. At the mile-and-one-half mark, my sides started to hurt. A few hundred yards from the finish, I thought I would collapse. Nothing comes easy, I told myself over and over again, and kept putting one exhausted foot in front of the other.

When I finally finished, I was super proud of myself. I looked up, gasping for breath, and saw an old man sitting on top of a hill. He'd been watching most of my run. He gave me a big smile and waved in congratulation.

Before going to the official training camp, I received a letter from the Cowboys telling me to make sure my feet were tough. I would be practicing twice a day, the letter said, and couldn't afford to lose time because of blisters. Countless players have failed to make it in the NFL because they missed practice time. The coaches absolutely will not baby you, no matter how much talent you think you might possess. If you can't practice, you can't play, and you're gone before you ever have a chance to show anyone what you can do.

Thousand Oaks training camp, on the campus of California Lutheran University, is forty-five miles north of Los Angeles. Although it can be beastly hot, the Cowboys train there because the weather is milder than the murderous Texas summer heat. The Houston Oilers train in Texas. I guess the Oilers figure the more brutal the weather, the better to get in shape. Landry figures if the weather is that bad, there won't be adequate time to practice.

Before going to Thousand Oaks, I read Jerry Kramer's book *Green Bay Packer Diary*. Kramer's descriptions of the toughness of training camp scared me—his remarks on the fanaticism of Vince Lombardi and especially on Lombardi's "grass drills." You run in place, Kramer said, fall on your face, leap up, run again, only to fall on your face again. Vince Lombardi could have passed for a sadist, but I found out Landry was worse than Lombardi.

Mom drove me out to Dallas's Love Field for the flight to California. "I'm scared," I told her. I really was. I didn't know what would happen to me if I didn't make the team.

"You'll be okay, Harvey," she said.

From Los Angeles we took a bus up to Thousand Oaks. There the rookies (the veterans wouldn't arrive for two weeks) were housed upstairs in a two-story dorm. By alphabetical assignment Drew Pearson and I ended up roommates again.

They gave us physicals the day we arrived, and then we ran. I thought we would never stop running. That first night there was a team meeting and then bed.

Rookie camp is pure hell. You hit and hit. You start hitting right away, first thing in the morning, and the coaches love it. They stand there and watch the players tear one another up. A player not in shape is lucky to last fifteen minutes of this. Fortunately, Joe Greene and Dwight White had warned me, and I came to camp in good shape, regardless of those thirteen pounds Stautner said I needed to lose. Also, I'd learned little tricks from Greene and White: how to break an offensive lineman's hold and how to use the headslap, which put me ahead of the others. I was the only one in camp who'd gotten this kind of help.

Unfortunately, the team doctor called me into his office after the first day of practice. "You've got something in your blood," he said. "You people have a blood disorder nobody else has. We're going to have to hold you out for a while."

Without knowing it, I had sickle cell anemia traits.

After that I spent all my time in my room, suffering more mentally than I ever could have physically with my teammates down on the practice field. Drew would drag himself into the room half dead and say, "You're lucky. Most of the guys are ready to collapse." But he and I both knew I wasn't lucky.

I did attend all the team meetings, and soon learned the Cowboy system was nothing like what I'd encountered as a high school or college player. In fact, it wasn't like anything anyone encountered as a pro in the NFL. Landry's system was so sophisticated, so complex, it was a wonder anyone could remember to block and tackle an opponent, as busy as he was trying to remember everything else he was supposed to do.

Meals were an agony for me. I felt like a fool at the Fat Man's Table. I'd always weighed 265. But Stautner wanted me at 252, and there was no appeal. Three days passed before the doctor told me I could practice—my condition was not life-threatening. At last I felt part of the team. The next day we scrimmaged against the Rams rookies.

One player, a second-year rookie (he'd been cut the year before), thought he knew some tricks of the trade. When this guy got too tired from running, he'd stick his finger down his throat and vomit. "Good way to keep yourself from collapsing, Harvey," he advised. The man didn't make it through his second rookie camp.

There were some eighty of us at rookie camp, a lot of bodies, and the Cowboys received much praise for being so democratic, for giving plenty of people a chance to make the team. Many of these rookies hung on until after the veterans arrived. But I learned what the Cowboys did wasn't such a good thing. Some of the rookies were kept on—and their hopes of making the team sadly kept alive— only as a target supply. Bob Lilly and Jethro Pugh needed someone big and warm to hit, and it wouldn't do if that someone were Roger Staubach.

After two weeks the veterans made the scene. Veterans don't talk to rookies. Veterans feel sorry for rookies, and they hate rookies. Veterans have families, wives, children. A rookie might take a veteran's job. Also, the rookie might not be around more than a day or two, so why waste time developing friendships?

I took part in a scrimmage with veterans the first week.
John Niland and Rayfield Wright were the pride of the
Cowboys offensive line. Two gigantic, rock-hard All-Pros,
they struck fear even in the hearts of established players.
On an early down in the scrimmage, Niland pulled out of
the line and hit me in the head with his helmet, raising a
knot on my skull the size of an orange. He literally bowled
me over. Niland and Rayfield were intentionally brutal,
exactly what the coaches ordered. The coaches wanted to
find out, and find out fast, which rookies could take it.

After that first scrimmage against Rayfield and Niland,
Ernie Stautner took me aside. "I don't know if you're
going to make the team," he said. "I don't think you're
tough enough."

I was shattered. I took a chance and went to see
Rayfield and Jethro Pugh and told them what Stautner had
said. "He might just be talkin'," Rayfield said. But neither
of them offered me much hope.

I figured time was running out and I'd better show
Coach Stautner how tough I really was. The next day
offensive tackle Bruce Walton, basketball star Bill
Walton's brother, pushed me after a play had ended. I
took a swing at him, knocked him down, jumped on him,
and hit him again. I wasn't mad at Walton; I wanted to
show Stautner I was tough. I guessed I'd succeeded when
I saw him smile. Looking back, I figure those two punches
I threw at Bruce Walton changed my football career.

John Niland provided us with some excitement when
we returned to Dallas from training camp, wandering
through a Dallas neighborhood and causing a disturbance.
The police were called. It took five of them plus two
neighborhood security guards to subdue the big offensive
guard. Some team veterans guessed Niland was high on
drugs. The official police version was that Niland had been
taken into custody "in his own best interest" because he
had been "acting suspiciously" and "talking inco-
herently."

Niland had a different explanation to explain why he had so abruptly left a friend's house, where he'd been watching TV:

When I left the house, I thought the Devil had hold of me. I thought my friends and my wife were part of a Devil-controlled people, and they were trying to take me into the cult as a member. I started running . . .

I was so close to death, I could feel it. I was possessed by the Devil. I accepted the fact I was going to die. I felt the Devil's temptation and I felt God's presence. To me, God was trying to tell me he wanted to help me.

Then I stopped running, and I started speaking in tongues [communication by control of the Holy Spirit]. God told me he wanted me to share my experience. He said He wanted me to pursue it [religion] with Iree [Niland's wife]. He said He wanted me to develop into a player-coach.

It was the perfect story for Coach Landry, a very religious man. At a team meeting the next day, Landry dismissed the episode: "John had a religious experience last night."

But Niland, my kind of guy (he had chutzpah), came up with other weird statements: "I was speeding so fast through life. The Devil had a hold of me. I was living in lust. I was living with women."

When Niland visited a psychiatrist, he knelt and said a prayer, then "gave his life to Christ." "Now I'm waiting to see what God wants me to do," he said.

Our first preseason game was the *Los Angeles Times* charity matchup against the Rams in the Coliseum. Landry called me into his room, the first of the four times in my eleven-year career with the Cowboys that he spoke to me. "You're going to play Saturday night," he said. "You've been making progress."

That amounted to the highest possible praise from

Landry, a man I believe is the finest football coach who ever lived.

I like to believe Landry spoke to me only four times because he knew I was doing my job. He didn't need to talk to me.

I don't think the Cowboys would ever lose a game, if they simply did exactly what Landry told them. Generally, Landry is not good at dealing with people as people, although I was an exception. He is like a great general, a master strategist, very cold and aloof; yet he genuinely loves and cares for his players. Still, the business side of him is like any other boss. If you're not doing the job, no matter how much he loves you, he'll replace you in the blink of an eye.

I came into the Rams game in the second quarter, early for a rookie. It was on a kickoff. I ran for the wedge like a maniac, tore down the coverage, knocked down the runner, and hurt my ankle. I didn't care. I didn't tell anyone I'd been hurt. I had endured too much pain getting into the game to let pain put me on the sidelines.

The next day the *Dallas Morning News* called me a "bright spot." Rodrigo Barnes, Billy Joe DuPree, and Drew were the other rookies who played that night. Drew returned punts and fumbled the first one that came his way. I felt almost as badly for him as he did.

The next punt he ran back 65 yards. Our great wide receiver Bob Hayes, an Olympic sprint champion and the fastest man in the world, had asked me earlier during a practice—I guess because I was standing there—"Who's Twenty-five?"

"Drew Pearson," I answered.

"Pretty good player," Hayes remarked.

Pretty good praise, coming from Bob Hayes.

*　　*　　*

It was terrible watching a player get cut from the team. I saw one rookie receive the news, begin crying, and then start breaking up furniture and throwing everything he could get his hands on. "They don't know what they're losing," he sobbed. "I'm a great player."

Soon some of the rooms on the second floor of the dorm had only one occupant, and others were empty. I know a rookie who walked into a singly occupied room and began to sit down on the bed. "Don't sit there," he was told. "The guy who slept in that bed got cut."

Before training camp ended, we had one more preseason game, against the Raiders in Oakland. The two Raiders tackles were Bob Brown and Art Shell, both over six feet six inches and 300 pounds. Brown's ugly face had been featured on the cover of *Sports Illustrated*, which advertised him as "the meanest tackle in pro football." Both Brown and Shell wore black gloves, and I wondered why.

I soon found out. *Every* down I played against Bob Brown, he clenched his fists and slugged me in the ribs.

It was in this game that I decided I didn't like my teammate Pat Toomay. Toomay claimed injury and said he couldn't play. I'll always believe he just didn't want to play against Art Shell. Toomay got replaced by Larry Cole, and this big-hearted man alternately went against both Shell and Brown, taking a terrible pounding. I looked at Toomay and thought, *I'm gonna get your job.*

I also went up against Art Shell this game, and he hit me in the head so hard that I found myself looking through the earhole of my helmet when I got up off the ground. Brown and Shell were two of the most vicious and effective offensive tackles I ever played against, the kind of men you wish were on your team.

But, as they say, my mama didn't raise a fool. I figured out real quick that I had to widen out against Brown, i.e., once he was set in position and unable to move again, I'd take a few steps outside and away from him. He was so big and I was so fast that there was no way he could catch me. As I perfected my techniques, I learned I loved to play against brutal assassins like Bob Brown.

I played almost the entire game against Oakland, thanks to Pat Toomay, and got bruises I figured would last a lifetime. My ribs ached terribly, and I feared a few of them had been broken.

Fortunately I had been hardened to take the abuse. One of the single most important factors in my development as an NFL player was that I practiced every day against Rayfield Wright. No matter who I faced on Sunday, he wasn't as tough, or as good, as Rayfield. Practices were always tougher for me than games.

We flew back to Dallas after the Oakland game. Mom and a girl friend met me at the airport. After a month of behaving myself, I wanted to see the girl friend more than Mom, but I didn't dare say so. "You look so skinny," Mom said when I got off the plane.

Landry announced, "Even though we're breaking camp, you're still in training camp."

Drew Pearson and I shared a Ramada Inn room. Happy as kids given keys to the candy store, Drew and I thanked the veterans who tipped us off that the coaches never pulled room check here.

Right.

I talked Drew into going to Balls with me. When we returned to the Ramada Inn, after curfew, there was a note from Coach Gene Stallings taped to the door.

At the next morning's team meeting, Landry announced dryly: "Two rookies were out late last night. One hundred and fifty dollars each."

A few nights later I went out again, figuring they'd never check a second time. When I returned, there stood Stallings, knocking on the door. At the meeting the next morning, Landry deadpanned: "Rookie out again last night. It was Martin. Three hundred dollars."

That payday my check, minus fines, came to

$0,000.00, thanks to the "tip" from the veterans. The Cowboys actually gave me a check for that non-amount.

I played a good exhibition game against the Kansas City Chiefs and overheard someone say I "hit as hard as Bob Lilly did as a rookie." Landry's judgment to the press was something different: "Harvey did okay, for a rookie."

Who makes the team? The Cowboys came down to their final few cuts and a lot of players, myself included (no matter that the numbers game told me I was in), lived in a state of extreme agitation and worry. I got the news via telephone call from my mother, who heard it on the radio. "Congratulations, Mr. Dallas Cowboy," she said.

We played our first regular season game against the Bears in Chicago. Many of our offensive players were afraid of Dick Butkus. I mean, flat-out scared. Butkus broke bones. Frankly, I'd never seen anything like him.

Butkus screamed all the time. "Fuck you, Ditka!" he'd yell at our special teams and tight end coach, now head coach of those same Bears. "I'm gonna break your neck." Butkus meant it.

Butkus is the only linebacker with fifteen straight minutes of highlight films showing him crushing one player after another. Players he hit complained the blows paralyzed them. Although the Cowboys team won this game against the Bears, Cowboy players lost plenty of individual battles to Butkus. I didn't see any action at all.

Gradually the coaches inserted me in third-down passing situations off the bench. Despite the extremely limited playing time, I led the entire team in sacks. Toomay didn't like it. But then, I didn't like his feeding me to Shell and Brown. I thought Toomay tried to avoid work and at times attempted to slip blocks instead of trying to run someone over.

The Cowboys were right not to play me on every down. Like everyone else, I had trouble learning the very complicated Flex defense. It's been said that by the time you truly understand the Flex, you're too old to play.

But by halfway through the season, fans in Texas Stadium would cheer and clap when I came in on third downs. I've always considered the Texas Stadium fans the best in the NFL, very refined and knowledgeable about football, more a symphony orchestra audience than a wrestling match crowd. Ours may not have been as loud as other crowds, but they weren't crude, like the throngs who watched in Washington, D. C., or the drunks who spat out obscenities in New England.

We won our first three games in 1973: 20–17 over the Bears, crushed New Orleans 40–3, and knocked out St. Louis 45–10.

In the fourth game of the season I got my first taste of the Redskins in RFK Stadium, a game we lost 14–7 when Kenny Houston stopped Walt Garrison on the 1-yard line on the last play of the game. Nobody, before or since, ever stopped Walt Garrison like that. The plane back to Dallas was a morgue, lights off all the way home.

I believe the Cowboy-Redskin rivalry is the fiercest in football, and some of our games against them undoubtedly rank among the most memorable ever played. Whenever we visited RFK we could always expect the nastiest remarks and waves of boos so loud that we couldn't hear the player introductions. I don't think the fans helped the Redskins, at least not against us. We wanted to shut them up real bad.

I came one vote short of making the All-Rookie team, beaten out by Barney Chauvous, who started for the Denver Broncos.

During the season, usually on Thursday nights, I'd visit H. P. Cassidy's, a nightclub on Greenville Avenue partly owned by quarterback Craig Morton. I'd sip a few beers and talk football with the regulars. It didn't take me

long, however, to feel that other blacks were being turned
away at the door.

It burned me that a black Cowboy football player
could walk into his establishment, but a black lawyer or
doctor couldn't. Presumably, a football player drew in
customers who wanted to watch. It wasn't long before I
pretty much stopped going into Morton's place.

I spent a lot of time during the season in Abner
Haynes's office, where something was always going on,
and at Balls, which attracted such celebrities as Stevie
Wonder and Earth, Wind and Fire.

At Abner's office I met his secretary, Sharon Bell, the
woman I came closest to marrying. This beautiful black
woman possessed all the poise and culture I lacked. She
was recently returned from Ethiopia, where she had lived
in a palace as a friend of a relative of Emperor Haile
Selassie. This worthy couldn't sleep with Sharon, so he
brought in a string of prostitutes. When Sharon found out,
she quickly split.

Sharon was the prettiest woman in Dallas, and I fell
hard for her. She also had brains. She explained restaurant
menus to me, and wine selections, and introduced me to
symphonies and live theatrical productions. A college
graduate, going for a postgraduate degree, Sharon came
from a wealthy San Francisco family. When her sister got
married, both the mayor of Oakland and the mayor of San
Francisco attended the wedding.

Sharon disliked football and didn't attend any games.
That she cared for me was flattering in the extreme. She
had princes interested in her, yet she liked me. We'd sit
around whole weekends just talking. And she gave me
freedom. She never said a word if I went out with the
boys. I thought her too good to be true.

The Cowboys made the NFC championship game my
rookie season. Just one step away from the Super Bowl,

we got blown out by the Minnesota Vikings 27–10. The Vikings drove us crazy with misdirection plays, dazzling runs by Chuck Foreman that kept us off balance the entire game.

Our locker room afterward was a tomb, a state that occurred again and again after defeats in my early years as a Cowboy. It was a sharp contrast to what came later.

The off-season of my 1974 sophomore year in the NFL was largely spent with Sharon Bell, who looked good to me compared to *everyone.* At this time I could go anywhere with Sharon and not be recognized—a wonderful situation, although I didn't appreciate our privacy at the time. After subsequent seasons people often looked at us, whispered, came over for autographs.

Most of the off-season talk among the Cowboy players centered on our first round draft pick, Ed "Too Tall" Jones, six feet nine inches and 285 pounds, a giant oak tree of a man—smart, lean, fast, quick, strong. Too Tall reportedly had amazing stamina and a tolerance for pain that defied imagination.

It all turned out to be true. Playing one of mankind's most violent games, Ed did not miss a single NFL contest *in twelve years.* Once, from the sidelines, I saw bones jutting through one of his fingers; the sight of it made me want to scream. But Too Tall went back on the field with the defense, never missing a down.

Ed Jones ranked First of the First in 1974, the first player chosen in the NFL draft. Usually a team selects a hotshot running back or quarterback, but the Cowboys, always more advanced in their thinking than other NFL teams, knew it was people like Too Tall who win Super Bowls. Not only did the selection of a defensive player surprise people, but so did his school of origin, virtually unknown Tennessee State.

My school, East Texas State, is another not mentioned in the same breath with Notre Dame and Ohio State. But the Cowboys were after players, not schools. Their scouting system, relying heavily on computers, had no peer. Cowboy management outsmarted other teams. In 1975, the Cowboys would pluck Thomas Henderson out of unknown Langston University in Oklahoma.

But that was the future. I had more immediate concerns.

"Ed Jones will take your job," I kept hearing after he got drafted Number One.

The hell he will, I thought, and searched him out on the practice field at the first opportunity. I realized right away I'd never seen a larger human being anywhere, but I plunged ahead. "You want to race?" I asked.

I won the contest, witnessed by a substantial number of players and coaches, and only much later realized I'd made a mistake. It's like being the fastest gun in the West. Having to accept the challenge of every hot-breathed kid who came into training camp was okay for a while (it seemed only fair, since Too Tall had raced me), but as the years mounted up I'd have preferred considering my position secure because of my experience.

But competing against Too Tall helped my career, even if he didn't compete against me. It was one of the factors that led me to All-Pro. I wanted to be as good as *he* was, and I worked exceedingly hard to be that good. I knew there would be an important position for me in football if I just came close to Too Tall's performance level.

It all worked out. Too Tall got put on one side of the defensive line, and I was put on the other. Many writers thought us the perfect pair of defensive ends. More important, Too Tall became one of my most cherished friends. I can't imagine a more valuable ally, on or off the field.

Friendship didn't stop my making bets with him that

he couldn't win. During the regular season preceding
Super Bowl XII against Denver, we wagered a six-pack of
beer a sack: If I made three sacks in a game, and he had
only one, he owed me two six-packs. Pride made the bet a
big deal. The payoff had to be in the Cowboy locker room
in front of all our teammates.

Even before the 1974 season started, signs cropped up
indicating that this would not be our finest year. The
World Football League contacted almost everyone on the
team, which produced a lot of rumbling that many of the
Cowboys intended to jump to the WFL. They called me
but I wasn't interested; I was living Camelot in my own
backyard.

The players union called a strike before the start of
training camp, and only one veteran, Ralph Neely, reported to Thousand Oaks. The principal issue in the
strike: Could a player negotiate with a number of pro
teams or was he bound to the franchise that drafted him?
Those most committed to the strike walked picket lines,
and I admired them for it. I spent most of my time with
Sharon; the days of my storied party-going had not yet
begun.

Since joining the Cowboys, I've always been very
active, almost constitutionally incapable of doing nothing.
During the off-season and the strike, I made appearances
at rattlesnake hunts, kissing competitions, and flagpole-
sitting contests. I willingly sought out events in out-of-the-
way places the big-name Cowboys wouldn't be found
dead at. I picked up some loose change, but often I made
appearances for free. I loved meeting young kids (I remembered what a thrill it had been for me when I saw Bob
Hayes), and besides, I felt it wouldn't hurt to become
better known.

To make matters less promising for the upcoming
season, friction cropped up on the team over the strike. It
couldn't have been any other way. For some, the issues at
stake were life-and-death. For others, they were minor

annoyances preventing them from collecting their regular paycheck.

I've always believed Coach Landry has the finest football mind I've ever encountered, but the only head coach the Cowboys have ever known also possessed his faults. He concentrated more on opponents than on his own team, so wrapped up with the game was he, so intent on discovering a weakness to exploit, and I don't think he realized the tensions that were building among his players.

To top everything off, the Cowboys had a quarterback controversy: Who would start, Roger Staubach or Craig Morton?

I didn't care. Mostly throughout my career I tried never to worry about the offense, who I hoped simply wouldn't *lose* the game for the defense. Besides, both Staubach and Morton were terrific players.

The rookies, not being members of the players union, reported on time to the Thousand Oaks training camp. I remained in Dallas worrying about Too Tall Jones getting a big jump on me during this vital period while I attended flagpole-sitting contests and listened to good music with Sharon Bell.

Gil Brandt gave me a call. "We sure would like you to come into camp," he said.

He wanted me to be a strikebreaker.

Brandt called me at a vulnerable time. I didn't feel secure in my position with the Cowboys and imagined all those hungry rookies, including the awesome Too Tall Jones, getting an impossible-to-overcome lead on me. Also, I got the impression that crossing the picket lines would lead to an upward renegotiation of my contract, which indeed proved to be the case. Despite that consideration, I wish now that I hadn't reported to camp.

The 1974 training camp was particularly brutal. Coach Landry feels a player needs so many two-a-days, so many sprints, so many miles, so many grass drills if he's to be ready for the grueling NFL season. Landry's got it all figured out in his head. And he's right. A player does need regimented conditioning, a lot of it.

A mountain towered over Thousand Oaks, and each morning before breakfast we "ran the mountain." Mike Ditka, then our assistant coach, qualified as a marathon runner, and he'd rouse us out of bed at daybreak to "race up" this mini-Everest. Coach Landry ran right along with us.

If you achieved a certain time running the mountain, you didn't have to do it the next day. I *never* won a day off. Trying to beat the magic time, however, I twisted my ankle, and in deference to my injury Landry had me run an endless series of hundred-yard sprints instead.

Getting me to work out, to practice hard, never posed a problem for anybody. The notion of hard work had long since been ingrained into my soul. And it made sense: Hard work had gotten me this far, after starting football so late.

Landry held what he called "concentration drills." Players lined up on each side of the ball and had to go the *instant* it got snapped. If you were either late or early, you lost. Losing meant you had to run 360 yards *after* practice, when all you really wanted to do was lie down and sleep forever. I had to run the 360 only once, and that time it wasn't my fault. A defensive back moved too quickly, but Coach Stautner thought it was me.

What about *his* concentration?

I always had great concentration. Coaches tell defensive linemen to go on the snap of the ball, but I never did. I went when the quarterback moved. Every quarterback makes some little movement just before the ball is snapped, and I watched endless films to discover that critical moment of movement. Often I arrived at the quarterback setup point simultaneously with the quarterback, yet I got whistled for offsides on pass-rushing downs very few times in my career. Most of these times I didn't go offsides. I believe officials called the penalties because they didn't believe I could legally get to the quarterback that fast.

I muttered and griped as I trudged off the field after doing my 360. "Harvey!" I heard Bob Lilly yell at me.

"Yeah?" I said, turning to face the future Hall-of-Famer.

"Cut out the complaining. Don't ever complain. You've got some talent, so just do the job." Good advice for a young player.

Every team needs players like Bob Lilly and Jethro Pugh—wise, hardened veterans who can show younger men the ropes. Of course, the younger athletes must be willing to listen, a problem for the Cowboys late in my career.

Bob Lilly taught me how to grab an offensive lineman's shoulder pad and pull him into me, and additional ways to break holds—a lifetime of tricks he'd learned in NFL trenches. This giant former TCU All-America, later known as "Mr. Cowboy," has been inducted into Texas Stadium's Ring of Honor.

Lilly played with the Cowboys almost from the beginning of the franchise's history, joining the team in 1961, the second year of the Cowboys. In his first season, Lilly hurt a knee, sprained both ankles, broke a thumb, a wrist, and five ribs, and still got named to the NFL All-Rookie team.

"In the latter stages of my career," he said, "I was rarely hurt, for the simple reason I finally knew what I was doing."

Lilly saw it all, from a 4–9–1 1961 season (the year before, the Cowboys were 0–11–1) to the glory of victory in Super Bowl VI over the Miami Dolphins.

I never tired of watching Bob Lilly, or learning from him. He could catch flies in midair with his right hand, then do it with his left, a feat requiring extraordinary quickness. I could do it with my right hand, but not with my left. I've read that former heavyweight champion Joe Louis could also catch a fly with either hand.

Lilly's legs were the talk of the locker room. He cut diamond-shaped holes in his practice uniform pants for ventilation, and his strange-looking diamond-studded sunburn came to about 20 carats total weight.

I also garnered valuable tips from Jethro Pugh, our 1965 eleventh-round draft pick out of Elizabeth City State. The forward-thinking Cowboys early on realized a player need not attend the likes of Penn State or USC to be a top prospect.

Jethro stood six feet seven inches and weighed 265 pounds. He became a father figure to his teammates, a nightmare for opponents. Technically the best player ever to man the defensive tackle position, Jethro experienced everything pro football had to offer. Ironically, the play many fans remember him for involved a mistake.

Jethro played in the 1967 NFL championship game, since dubbed the Ice Bowl, against the Packers in Green Bay. It was one of football's most memorable contests. The Packers, with no times out left, owned the ball on the Dallas 1-yard line with thirteen seconds to go. Everyone who witnessed it remembers the block Jerry Kramer made on Jethro, permitting Bart Starr's sneak into the end zone. The play has been shown literally thousands of times on highlight films, and I've studied it on numerous occasions.

Jethro made one of the few errors of his football life that day, although his version—and he was on the field—is different. I believe Jethro set himself up just a fraction too high. Down on the goal line a defensive lineman needs to get as low as possible in the root hog position, so named for the pig who sticks his snout in the mud.

"It was a good play on Starr's part," Jethro remembers. "He hadn't run a quarterback sneak all season. But to this day I still maintain that Kramer was offsides. As far as that goes, [center Ken] Bowman actually got better contact on me on the play."

Jethro also had the bad luck of spending much of his career next to Bob Lilly, who got all the press.

The younger Cowboys knew Jethro as a strong, quiet leader. No matter how stressful the situation, we could count on his never making a foolish error, never being caught out of position. It hurts a team to worry about covering for another player; with Jethro we didn't. We just knew he'd do the right thing. Line coach Ernie Stautner, a perfectionist, featured Jethro at clinics to demonstrate proper technique.

Jethro had one regret: "There was one thing I always wanted to do that I never managed to accomplish—I wanted to play the perfect game. I came close a few times, but after a while I realized it was impossible to do. Still, it was a good goal to shoot for all those years."

Indeed. Players like Lilly and Pugh made the Cowboys the great team they were. No wonder they thought they could call Coach Landry "Tom."

The Cowboys kept seven defensive linemen in 1974: Pat Toomay, Larry Cole, Jethro Pugh, Bill Gregory, Bob Lilly, Too Tall Jones, and me.

Once again I played mostly on third-down pass rushing situations, but I still managed to lead the team in sacks. The Texas Stadium crowd cheered whenever Too Tall or I came into a game, a vote of confidence I hoped might persuade Landry to put us in the starting lineup. But I knew Landry would make us regulars when, and only when, he judged us ready.

Later in my career, on the big Texas Stadium scoreboard, the word *MARTINIZED* flashed across the screen each time I made a sack. I loved it. I wanted to see it appear after every play.

I simply ate up most offensive tackles. I had too much speed for them. As I've mentioned, it helped enormously that I practiced every day against Rayfield Wright.

The Cowboys finished 8–6 in 1974, and for the only time in my eleven-year career we didn't make the play-offs. Tension on the team was terrific. Lots of guys had signed with the WFL, and some were not putting out for fear of sustaining an injury that would hamper them in the new league.

We'd lost the brilliant, mercurial running back Duane Thomas, and Calvin Hill had already made plans to go to the WFL. Bob Hayes was older, and 1974 became his last season with the Cowboys. Hayes literally had been the fastest man in the world, and the best big play receiver the Cowboys ever had. Hayes, by himself, caused a major change in pro football. He simply ran too fast for any defensive back to cover him, so coaches designed what became the present-day zone defense, where a defender covers an *area*, not a player.

In 1967 Bob Hayes averaged an incredible 26.1 yards per catch. In a game against the Oilers he caught four touchdown passes, each one for more than 40 yards. He was a great punt returner; his 90-yarder against Pittsburgh still stands as the Cowboy record. When the Cowboys released Hayes at the end of the 1974 season, it caused considerable grumbling among many of the veteran players—and among some of the younger ones, including me. Even if Hayes had slowed down, we felt he still towered head and shoulders above his replacement, Golden Richards.

Drew Pearson shone as the bright spot of our 1974 year. He caught more than sixty passes.

The combination of the strike, players leaving for the WFL, and internal dissension left a sour taste in most of our mouths. The good part was that everyone determined to make it all the way to the Super Bowl next year.

*   *   *

Shortly after the season ended, a friend of mine approached me. "I've got a deal for you," he said.

"What?" I said.

"Sapphires," he said.

"What?"

The deal required $50,000 to finance a sugar transaction. Sugar prices had shot sky-high at this time, and I was told the money would be used to bribe Mexican officials to grease the way for the shipment of vast amounts of scarce sugar. My friend came to me because he knew I sought potential investments.

It turned out that two California businessmen, considered to be very religious, were offering to pay back $150,000 in six months for the $50,000 loan. As collateral they put up a $400,000 sapphire collection, which would belong to whoever loaned the money, if it wasn't repaid. I put up $15,000, and the balance was contributed by Rayfield Wright, Abner Haynes, Glen Holloway (of the Bears), and Andre Tillman.

My lawyer flew to Los Angeles and met with the two businessmen. He picked a jeweler at random out of the Yellow Pages to make an appraisal of the stones. The jeweler set their value at $400,000 and signed a notarized statement attesting to their worth.

Six months later, with the loan in default (it turned out the religious guys had conned a number of people), Glen Holloway and I flew to Los Angeles to get the stones, which had been left in a bank safety deposit box. We took the gems to another appraiser, who glanced at them and said, "Indian sapphires. They're worthless."

I still don't know how the scam got pulled. My lawyer had selected the jeweler at random. How did the con men know which jeweler would be chosen?

Fortunately, the jeweler was still in business, and my lawyer went after him. Rayfield Wright helped pay the lawyer's fees, which mounted steadily, and also loaned me money to keep me going.

The $15,000 I'd lost had been a heavy blow, and my investment in Balls wasn't paying off either. The nightclub ultimately went out of business.

I'll always be grateful to Rayfield for the help he gave me. Glen Holloway, Andre Tillman, and Abner Haynes, thinking the cause hopeless, refused to pay anything to the lawyer. Rayfield and I, after a two-year legal hassle (a United States marshall first had to seize $400,000 worth of the jeweler's own gems), finally got our money back, with a slight profit. I couldn't grieve that our partners never saw a dime. They had a chance to pursue the case and passed it up.

But Balls and the sugar deal represented only minor forerunners to investments that would go bad for me as I sought to provide myself a livelihood after football.

Needing money following the 1974 season, I took a job selling shoes in a store owned by the Zale Corporation. It didn't bother me. I wasn't too proud, and besides I had good company—Drew Pearson sold sporting goods equipment in the same place.

I sold shoes and attended events no other Cowboy wanted, like armadillo races, and looked forward to a big year in 1975. Pat Toomay had gone to the WFL, although I would have started this next season anyway. I was ready.

6

ince I was a veteran, I wasn't at Thousand Oaks to view the arrival of Thomas "Hollywood" Henderson and the other rookies for training camp in 1975. But all of us would get to know Thomas soon enough.

He admitted later in a national magazine article that he checked into the dormitory on the first day carrying a couple of hits of THC, some reefer, and some acid. His attitude, even at the beginning, although he kept this from me for a long time, was that he didn't have to learn, Landry had nothing to teach him; he knew it all. Henderson believed football required athletic skills and an ability to knock the other guy out of his shoes—nothing more—and by God, Hollywood could do these things.

Thomas Henderson unquestionably ranks as the most talented linebacker ever to play the game, and also the most troubled.

He was born and grew up in Austin, Texas, where his mom and stepfather eked out a precarious existence. At age twelve he saw his mother shoot and seriously wound his stepfather with a .22 caliber rifle during a domestic spat caused by drinking. Soon thereafter Thomas began picking up pocket money by burglarizing homes. In his early teenage years, he popped pills, drank Robitussin, smoked reefer, and snorted heroin. A marvelous physical specimen with spectacular athletic skills, Thomas usually remained ineligible to play school sports because of failing grades. Somehow he wangled a football scholarship to Langston University, a small black school in Langston, Oklahoma, where he became a Little All-American. In college he had all the girls and drugs he wanted, and that was a lot.

The Cowboy computers early on spotted this rare, once-in-a-lifetime talent. But the computers could only measure athletic statistics, not a man's character.

Henderson was drafted Number One by the Cowboys. The same day he walked into a car dealership, identified himself as a first-round draft choice, and walked out with a new Corvette without even making a down payment.

Other Cowboy linebackers—Mike Hegman, Bob Breunig, D. D. Lewis—thought Henderson was too slow to learn the system, or that he didn't try. "But it wasn't that I couldn't learn the system," said the man who became known as Hollywood. "I just didn't want to learn it, because I already knew I could play."

While Henderson may have thought he didn't need to work out, that's about all I did in the months leading up to the 1975 season. During lunch break from selling shoes, I'd hustle over to the Cowboy training center to lift weights and run sprints. I needed to build my strength, since I was smaller than most of the offensive linemen paired against me. I accumulated twenty sacks during my first two seasons, and now I dedicated myself to becoming the best pass rusher in the game.

In 1975 Coach Landry made the brilliant decision to start Ed Jones and me at the two defensive end positions. Too Tall would play the strong side (left) defensive end, because most offensive teams are right-handed and run in that direction. I played right side defensive end, which allowed me to free-lance a great deal and set up numerous opportunities for sacks. Too Tall played stronger against the run; I played stronger against the pass.

D. D. Lewis played outside right linebacker behind me, and he'd call "Jet," meaning an outside charge, or "Fly," a head-up rush right through the offensive tackle's nose. I'd hit the tackle, hold him, slide away, clothesline the blocking back, and take exquisite enjoyment watching D.D. tear the terrified quarterback to pieces. Being switched to right defensive end meant I didn't go head-to-head against Rayfield in practice.

I always closely watched the top draft choices of the Cowboys to see if any of these new studs could help us. Right away I knew Thomas Henderson could. He ran 100 yards in 9.5—faster than all but the speediest backs—and hit like a tractor-trailer. At this time Thomas impressed me as a nice kid, delighted to be a Cowboy, as I always was. He was pleasant to be around, except that he invariably introduced himself with, "I'm Thomas Henderson, Dallas Cowboys' Number One draft choice." This bothered me—he didn't have to blow his horn this way—but I shrugged it off.

I tried to show him the ropes, the "veteran" taking the kid aside, telling him how it is. Thomas acted as if he already knew. He wouldn't listen to anyone. I'd never met a person so in love with himself. Me, Me, Me was his unceasing credo, but he possessed prodigious ability, and perhaps the Cowboys computers didn't have to see more than that.

I will say this: Whenever Thomas met my mom or any other member of my family, he always showed the greatest respect. At those times he became a different person.

But Henderson wasn't the only Cowboy I kept my eye on. The 1975 Cowboy draft probably qualifies as the finest any team ever had. An unprecedented twelve rookies—nicknamed the Dirty Dozen—made the team, among them Scott Laidlaw, Pat Donovan, Herb Scott, Randy White, Bob Breunig, and Randy Hughes. This bumper crop of rookies came at just the right time. Bob Lilly, Walt Garrison, and Cornell Green had retired.

Immediately I could tell that Randy White would be something special. At six feet three inches and 260 pounds, Randy was—is—one of the strongest men in the world, but what set him apart from others was his intensity. He was *always* coming, first play of the game to last. Opponents who figured Randy might let up in the fourth quarter of a lopsided game got seriously injured. He went all-out every down.

Fighting with an opponent on the field is hardly uncommon, but how about with your own teammate during a regular season game? I once made a mistake defensing a running play and suddenly found Randy in my face, screaming and cursing. "Fuck off, Randy!" I said. We squared off to do battle, then simultaneously realized it would be ludicrous. Besides, no Cowboy would get between us, and the risk of injury was too high. Certainly the opposing Redskins would only stand around and enjoy.

Randy joined Too Tall, Hollywood, and me for some serious partying early in his career, although he slowed down after he got married. This incredibly muscular and powerful individual, known to the football world as Manster—half man, half monster—is in reality a bigger-than-life good-ole-boy character who could have come straight out of Pete Gent's bestselling *North Dallas Forty*.

Cowboy management immediately recognized Randy as the perfect employee. He worked hard all day, came back the next day, and did it again. I've seen him bench press 475 pounds and pick up opposing running backs as easily as the average person might lift a five-pound sack of sugar.

Bob Breunig, a 260-pound All-America linebacker out of Arizona State, played under Frank Kush in college, which meant he had to be tough. Kush, an exacting taskmaster in the Woody Hays mold, wouldn't accept anything less, and rumors held that Breunig had been a favorite of his.

Randy Hughes, a defensive back from the University

of Oklahoma, was sometimes plain crazy, an early indication he'd be a helluva football player. Once a week a deli would send over a big cake for the players, and Hughes would stick his whole face into it.

"The Beautiful Harvey Martin Show" got born during 1975 training camp. It was the brainchild of network sportscaster Frank Gleiber, who'd heard me speak several times on radio. Whenever I went on the air I waxed eloquent. I worked at it. It embarrassed me to hear some players in front of a microphone sounding like meatheaded dumbbells, constantly saying "uh," "you know," "like." Often these were intelligent men, but they sounded foolish.

"We'd like you to do three shows a week for KRLD," Gleiber said. "You can answer questions from Al Wick. Is $20 a show good enough?"

"Sure."

I'd been giving interviews for free.

"How about doing five shows?"

"Sure."

"How would you like your own show?"

"Sure."

And that's how "The Beautiful Harvey Martin Show" came to life. It eventually became the most listened-to show in Dallas, five minutes a program and airing several times throughout the day. I tried to tell fans what they wanted to know: What's it like in training camp? Answer: Terrible. How does Roger's arm really feel?

Later on I caught some heat from Cowboy management about the show, because what the fans wanted to know involved more than what Cowboy management wanted them to know.

When Clint Longley and Danny White were backup quarterbacks for Roger Staubach, I told a story on "The Beautiful Harvey Martin Show" that quickly made national headlines.

Longley was my kind of guy: wacky. He had a house

on Lake Ray Hubbard, where he kept a cannon that he shot off at irregular intervals. He stocked guns and knives everywhere, and once cleared out the Cowboy locker room when he brought a sack of rattlesnakes inside. In short, he was nuts.

But Landry's bag was winning, not personalities, and as long as "Mad Bomber" Longley had that arm, the Cowboys' head coach figured he might help the team. (Landry, incidentally, despite speculation to the contrary, doesn't have a racist bone in his body. All he sees is a player's ability, nothing else.) However, Longley believed Landry favored the clean-living, very religious Danny White over his own rather wild ways. In reality, the problem existed only in Longley's imagination. Nevertheless, pressure built up inside him. Everything came to a head at the end of one long, tiring practice, when Clint threw a pass to Drew, who missed it.

"Catch the ball, you skinny fucker," Longley shouted at Drew.

"Clint," remonstrated Roger Staubach, "that's enough. You've been awful to live with. You don't talk at meetings. All you do is sulk."

"Let's go over to the bushes and settle this," said Longley.

"Okay," said Roger.

I thought it hilarious. I always liked a good fight, although this one turned out one-sided. Roger, a tough dude, would have hurt Longley much worse than he did if others, myself not included, had failed to intervene.

I began my next radio show: "Defensive linemen and offensive linemen aren't the only ones who fight. Roger Staubach and Clint Longley. . . ."

It caused a tremendous to-do in Dallas, and the story soon spread all over the country. Cowboy management, always concerned with image, thought it would have been better if the story had gone unreported. But management's negative reaction registered as nothing compared to Clint Longley's. He was hot because I'd said Roger had won the fight.

Clint came into the locker room boiling mad. Roger was putting on his shoulder pads, which meant his arms were pinned, and Longley slugged him. Roger fell back, hitting his head on the weight scale, and for a minute everyone thought we had lost our star quarterback. Longley left. High-ups in the Cowboy organization looked around for someone to blame for the scandal and possible injury to the irreplaceable Roger. They found me.

Tex Schramm rightly concerns himself with the Cowboy image and, recently, especially where drugs are concerned. But sometimes I can't help thinking something of a double standard is at work here. For example, Schramm knew management personnel consumed a lot of liquor at Thousand Oaks, but he didn't talk about that.

After the Longley-Staubach affair Schramm was saying loudly that he would lay down the law to me about what I could say on my radio show.

I went to him before he could call me in on the carpet. "Mr. Schramm," I said, "I'm sorry I caused the Cowboys any embarrassment; that's one of the last things I want to do. I'm sorry. But please understand, I'm a defensive lineman, and things like this little lightweight fight are nothing to me."

"I know," Schramm said. "It's okay. But I want to talk to you in my office when we get back to Dallas."

I figured it best to confront the situation right then. "Is it about my radio show?" I asked. "Are you going to tell me to give up my radio show?"

I knew Paul Brown in Cincinnati had made Bob Trumpe abandon his show, and the result had been a scandal—"Why?" people wanted to know. "Can't a player talk?" Maybe that was in Tex Schramm's mind when he told me he would not ask me to make changes on the show.

Longley was soon gone from the Cowboys. No one's

value to the team was sufficient to risk injury to Roger. Rumor had it that Longley, carrying a gun, came looking for Staubach afterward. Whether that was so or not, the Mad Bomber was something else. He once wrecked his car driving from Oklahoma to Dallas at 100 m.p.h., and then bragged that he survived despite the fact the vehicle had been crammed full of fireworks. As far as the game went, Terry Bradshaw and Jim Hart could throw a football farther than anyone I've ever seen, but Longley didn't lag far behind.

At training camp the players drank beer, management drank liquor. One front office guy almost died from liver problems caused by alcohol. The coaches, following Landry's example, drank nothing. I never saw Landry take a drop.

Everyone, myself included, viewed Director of Player Personnel Gil Brandt as shrewd, if not a wizard. The 1975 draft, for which he could largely take credit, strengthened his reputation as a genius.

Gil saved the hide of a lot of players. He could always keep the damage from a DWI arrest to a minimum, or a player out of jail if he tore up a bar. Players who got behind with payments to banks learned Gil could get them an extension, and he always knew the best places to buy TVs, furniture, and cars. Gil even found babysitters for the married players.

"We'll take care of you, if you take care of us," Gil said. And to a large extent, it was true.

A dedicated football player—and you'd better be dedicated if you played for Landry—simply didn't have time to take care of all his everyday needs. My own day started at 9 A.M. with a shower and getting dressed. Then it was out to the practice field at 10, and a heavy workout until 11:30. From 11:30 till noon there would be a special team meeting. Twelve to 1 P.M. was lunch (many players, myself included, skipped eating to conduct business during this hour). From 1 to 3 there were more team meetings. From 3:30 to 5:30 we had full-scale practices.

After a shower and treatment for various injuries, it was 6:30 before I left, and then at home from 7:30 to 8:30 I watched films of my next week's opponents. Specifically, I watched *every* movement of the quarterback, the offensive linemen I'd be up against, and the blocking back. At this time, except for our quarterbacks, I was perhaps the only player who did this sort of film study, but when I became the most successful sacker in the league, other players began to emulate me. Since there weren't enough films to go around, I had to become adept at keeping hold of those that were available.

From 8:30 to whenever on Thursdays and Fridays—but never the night before a game—I partied. I still hadn't hit my full stride in the having-fun department, but I enjoyed going to clubs for beer and picking up young women.

One thing that struck me as sad, and it became sadder to watch as the years went by, was seeing a veteran released from the team. Before the 1975 season started, I observed our great defensive back Cornell Green walking away from Landry's office, head down, with a terrible look of dejection on his face.

"Hey, Corny, what's going on?" I asked. He kept moving as if he hadn't heard me. The Cowboys said Cornell Green retired, but I still believe Landry told him they didn't need him anymore.

Cornell and I had enjoyed good times together—talking quietly, drinking beer, eating ham hocks. "Harvey can play with me," this great veteran had said of me when I was a rookie and needed encouragement.

The new-look Dallas Cowboys added still another new player in 1975, although he was anything but a rookie. When I heard the Cowboys had signed Preston Pearson, I thought, "Oh, wow!"

The Steelers really messed up when they let Preston go. Preston Pearson had already played in two Super Bowls, with the Baltimore Colts in Super Bowl III and with the Steelers the year before. He added stability and toughness to our team at the key running back position. Preston was a great physical specimen—lightning out of the blocks—and had wonderful moves. He excelled as a running back who could catch passes. And how he could catch them! Preston could always get open, even when Drew couldn't. He added wisdom and experienced leadership to our rookie-laden club. The first night Preston came to Dallas, Too Tall and I showed him the night spots.

I welcomed this new era. Nobody wanted trouble like 1974. We had an excellent mesh of "babies" and veterans, and I thought we might go all the way.

My own role model was Lee Roy Jordan, linebacker from Alabama and All-Pro. Jordan was a holler guy, always full of fire, tough as steel. Lee Roy, another of what I'd call the old-time players, never gave up, and he was a terrific hitter. He could break a leg and still come limping after you on the other.

Most Cowboy connoisseurs consider 1975 Landry's greatest coaching year, and rightly so. He didn't yet have the best talent in the NFL; that still remained a year or so away. But what the Cowboys couldn't do with sheer ability, Landry accomplished with trickery. He introduced the shotgun offense and fine-tuned what already were the most sophisticated offense and defense in the league.

We won our first four regular season games, then lost 0–4 to Green Bay, proving to my mind that *any* NFL team can defeat any other. The differences between personnel are very slight. The worst teams in the NFL have players who starred in college and will happily pound the hell out of you if you let them. Much of a losing team's problem is mental—they don't think they can win, therefore they can't. A good opposing team never allows them to believe otherwise.

In the seventh game of the regular season, a 30–24 overtime loss to the Redskins at RFK, I suffered my first major injury. I was convinced it was intentionally inflicted. Redskin tight end Jackie Smith (not the Jackie Smith who later played with the Cowboys) rammed his helmet into my ankle. The sprain hurt so badly that I couldn't walk, and I vowed the next time I saw Jackie Smith, I'd get revenge.

I started in the next week's game against Kansas City, but then couldn't continue. Randy White took my place. He played excellently.

The following week I didn't start against New England. I thought I would pass out from the excruciating pain in my ankle. That was the only game in my career I didn't start once I became a regular.

I'd become very cocky—crazy, some people would say—thinking I could do anything, which is how a defensive lineman should feel. Certainly I loved the attention success brought.

However, I began to think I couldn't take much more of Ernie Stautner's attention. I never answered him back, although he was always screaming at me. "I did it to bring out the best in Harvey," he later insisted.

But I never felt that his yelling motivated me, and I was the only player he screamed at. I told Sharon Bell, my confidante, that very soon I might have to go head-to-head with Ernie.

"Harvey, you're not doing it right," Stautner kept telling me. But I got the job done, better than almost anyone else in football, although my technique wasn't the best. The Cowboys had the most structured of defenses, and I wasn't always where I should be.

"He's driving me crazy," I complained to Sharon at night.

"Talk to him," she advised.

"Don't talk to him," Too Tall Jones advised. "Don't let him get to you. Just take it."

"Take it," Jethro Pugh counseled. "He's the coach."

One day at the end of practice, Stautner picked players to cover the kicking team. This was a job that starters didn't do. Stautner knew I was exhausted and suffering with the sore ankle, but just the same he told me to get out there and cover the kicks. I limped out onto the field.

"You don't want Harvey," Toni Fritsch, our kicker, said to Stautner. "I'll do it."

"Thanks, man," I said gratefully to Fritsch.

Evidently Stautner hadn't heard. When he saw Fritsch out on the field, he glared at me. "I said *you*, Harvey!"

I wanted to pound him. Instead I went out on the field. I knew Stautner wouldn't do this to Too Tall.

Still, to win together we had to live together. I kept my mouth shut. I kept it shut too much. I didn't talk during defensive meetings; I didn't contribute anything. I merely sulked.

I realized this wasn't doing any good either. Our goal was to win, and I never doubted Stautner wanted that, too. One day, to break the ice, I spoke up, asking Ernie a question about the defense that I already knew the answer to. Stautner seemed very pleasantly surprised. He and I then became friends, and his shouting let up a little, but not much. He still yelled at me about my technique.

The next-to-last game of the season, we met the Redskins in Texas Stadium. I had two goals: to beat Washington and to club hell out of Jackie Smith. I accomplished both. We routed the Redskins 31–10, and I came close to hospitalizing Smith. I went after him on every down, clubbing him with my forearms, punching him hard in the rib cage with my fists. The message wasn't just to him alone. I didn't want anyone to think they could deliberately injure me and get away with it.

Our last game of the regular season was against the Jets and Broadway Joe Namath in New York City. My plan was to knock Joe Namath out of the game—smash him silly, make certain he couldn't play another down. I succeeded.

Namath, backpedaling, fell on his back. I had gotten by the offensive tackle and came forward in the middle of a full charge. Terror flashed in Namath's eyes. He held his hands up and mouthed, "No, no." He was helpless as a rag doll.

Should I? I thought for just an instant.

Pow!

I hit him hard, driving my helmet and shoulder pads into him. He didn't get up, and I knew we'd seen the last of Broadway Joe for the day.

Some football fans didn't like the hit, but it was perfectly legal. Namath himself will tell you: Do anything legal you can to win the game. What if I'd backed off? He could have gotten up. Football's a tough game and Namath knows it.

In the divisional playoffs we defeated the Minnesota Vikings 17–14 in Minnesota, thanks to one of the greatest catches of all time, the "Hail, Mary" reception by Drew Pearson in the last seconds. The Vikings had been heavily favored against the wild-card Cowboys, and when Drew caught the ball one-handed, his hand down by his hip, I went wild with joy, racing out on the field to hug my roommate.

Before that impossible catch, I'd felt miserable on the sidelines, the only time in my entire career I thought we'd lost a game before it was over. The Cowboys outplayed the Vikings all afternoon, but until Drew's heroics, we seemed doomed to lose.

After catching the ball, Drew threw it high in the air, making it soar, like our hopes, all the way up against the Metropolitan Stadium scoreboard behind the end zone.

Unfortunately, the crowd also went wild. Their basic emotion was anger. A bottle hurled onto the field after Drew's catch hit an official on the head and knocked him out. Other objects rained onto the field, and for a while I thought the fans would pour out of the stands and attack us.

The next week in Los Angeles in the NFC championship game we crushed the favored Rams 37–7, and Preston Pearson set a playoff record with three touchdown receptions.

So off we went to Florida and Super Bowl X against the defending world champion Pittsburgh Steelers. Nobody gave us much of a chance, but then, they hadn't been giving us much of a chance all year. The experts just didn't understand what a great coaching job Landry had done with his dirty dozen rookies, nor that Too Tall and I had emerged as dominant defensive players. We couldn't know it at the time, of course, but the appearances of Too Tall and myself in 1975 coincided with the winningest five-year period in Cowboy history.

Our percentage between 1975 and 1979 was .756: fifty-six wins and eighteen losses. All five years we went to the playoffs. Four times we were NFC East champions. And three times we went to the Super Bowl. Along with the Steelers, we were the dominant team of the decade. Unlike the Steelers, we really *were* America's team, with fans everywhere in the United States.

Defense—the feared Steel Curtain—came to mind when people thought about the Steelers. Although I didn't have to worry about their defense, I knew I had to get to Terry Bradshaw and knock him out of the game. I understood very well what Roger and my friends faced trying to score against Pittsburgh. Quite simply their front four— L. C. Greenwood, Ernie Holmes, my old friend Mad Dog White, and Mean Joe Greene—was the roughest, meanest (some, but not me, would add dirtiest) ever to play the game. The Steeler front four was a violent, semicrazed wrecking crew.

Ernie Holmes wasn't semicrazed. He seemed to me to be all the way gone. His teammates called him Fats, but he really was a monster: six feet two inches and 290 pounds, with a passion to maim. In one sitting he could drink two fifths of cognac, a liquid that didn't give him a pleasant high. A mean, nasty drinker, his eyes usually blazing with hatred, he left no doubt that he'd cheerfully remove your head. Some players were afraid of Ernie Holmes, who could inflict major hurt on even the biggest opponents. This violent, crazy man had a tough girl friend, too. When Ernie cut his hair in the shape of an arrow, so did his girl—Ms. Arrowhead.

Mean Joe Greene didn't evoke many laughs from the players who had to go up against him either. Mean Joe stood six feet four inches, and his body was so thick he could rightly be called a colossus. If he got angry, a state usually precipitated by his team's lagging score, he could become vicious. A nationwide TV audience once saw him drive his right fist into the rib cage of a Denver Bronco, a blow I thought could have killed the man. Like Ernie Holmes, Joe possessed nearly supernatural strength, and he could literally run over and through opponents. Unlike Ernie Holmes, Joe was a gentle person off the field and a good friend to me.

L. C. Greenwood, all six feet seven inches of him, is now seen regularly on TV crushing Miller Lite cans and uprooting trees for former quarterback Bert Jones. In the Steelers' scheme of things back in the seventies, he served as pass rusher extraordinaire. Greenwood had a tremendous straight-ahead charge. The Cowboy offensive line had their hands full keeping him off Roger's back.

Then there was Dwight "Mad Dog" White, my old college roommate. His nickname really fit him. Dwight hailed from Dallas and especially hated the Cowboys, but he pulled out all the stops to win against any team. He would spit in an opponent's face, slug him, knee him—a rough man in a rough game. I'd wanted to wear Dwight's number, 78, but it was taken by Bruce Walton when I joined the Cowboys.

The year before I'd gone to Tulane Stadium and seen the Steelers beat the Vikings in Super Bowl IX, one of the most lopsided games ever played. I understood football, otherwise I would have felt pity for the Vikings. There they were, getting beat up, mugged, in front of tens of millions of people. The Steeler defense, a collection of eleven Rambos, beat on a weaker opponent. I think it helped me to watch that game in New Orleans. It gave me an idea of how loud the crowd noise would be. The sound seemed like a physical thing—able to pick you up and carry you right over the top of the stadium.

The Steelers were the toughest kids on the block, and they intended to break the bones of all those pretty faces on America's team. Their attitude toward us was one of genuine disdain. They thought most of the Cowboys were sissies and never tired of saying so. This was typical pregame hype.

Super Bowl X was played in the Orange Bowl in Miami. We stayed at a lovely beachfront hotel in Fort Lauderdale, and the place was mobbed by the media. No matter what I did, someone snapped my picture. I felt like Cinderella and hoped that after the game I wouldn't find myself back in the ashes. Mom, Dad, and Sharon (even she couldn't pass up a football game like the Super Bowl) came to Miami for the game, and I knew either I or the Steelers would eat some humble pie.

I didn't intend to be humiliated in front of the people I loved the most, yet that's just what the wicked stepmother Steelers said they'd do to us.

One evening some six days before the game, I went out to dinner with Billy Joe DuPree and another teammate, and when we returned to the hotel lobby, an absolutely gorgeous young woman approached us and stared at us. Our teammate seized the opportunity. He learned: (1) she came from Dallas; (2) she liked the Cowboys; (3) she made her living as an exotic dancer; and (4) she was looking for fun. We took her up to the room I shared with our teammate, which alone would have caused Landry to blow a gasket. But as they say, you ain't seen nothin' yet. The well-endowed dancer performed a very seductive striptease and then she and he headed for the bedroom.

At the last minute, he backed off, telling her the truth: He was married. She asked if I knew anyone else. I did.

The player I recommended must not have been enough for her, although he certainly wouldn't want to hear this. In any case, having satisfied him, the bouncy young miss asked for another player . . . and then another. I sat out in the living room of the suite, amazed, as a long line of players went in and out of that bedroom. I stopped counting when more than half our roster had entered and left. The dancer could go back to Dallas and truly say she had made the Dallas Cowboys football team.

The next day she left, disappeared. I never heard of anyone seeing her again, which at least for the moment seemed a good thing, because up ahead of us lay the toughest football game of our lives.

I was suffering from a bruised thigh, an injury that recurred throughout my career. This time it was due to an airborne Dave Edwards missing a tackle and crashing into my leg with his helmet. My leg swelled up to enormous proportions. Because of the thigh injury, I could only practice a few days, since practice aggravated the condition.

As always, Landry's preparations were very thorough. He told us he believed we could beat the Steelers, despite their implying that we wore kneepants and beanies.

I never doubted Coach Landry. As I've said, I believe

he knew other teams even better than his own. If he thought we could beat Pittsburgh, we could.

What you saw with the Steelers, Landry told us, was what you got. They did nothing subtle; we didn't have to worry about their tricking us or about their adding new wrinkles on offense or defense to throw us off. They'd come out hitting, hoping to injure and maim. Landry could be counted on *always* to be right in such matters. I knew if we lost this game, it wouldn't be because the Steelers surprised us. We had to be ready for a war, hand-to-hand combat.

Of course, we had to match Steeler toughness with Cowboy toughness, but we weren't just going to leave it at getting down in the pigsty mud and wallowing with them all afternoon. We'd gotten to the Super Bowl in large part because of our brains—our state-of-the-art offense and defense—and we had some tricks waiting for the Stone Age Steelers.

One controversial point Landry emphasized before the game: We were not to allow the Steelers to provoke us into fights. The Steelers *wanted* to fight. Landry, the perfectionist, felt fighting would take away from the concentration we needed, besides which brawling could draw costly penalties. Let the Steelers be penalized, he said.

Preston Pearson, who had been on the Steelers Super Bowl IX championship team, thought this advice wrong. He believed that if we didn't retaliate against the Steelers' ultra-rough tactics, they'd raise the level of violence several notches and pound us to death.

We showed the Steelers Cowboy brains on the opening kickoff. Using language you wouldn't hear in a Singapore brothel, the Steelers came thundering down the field intent on decapitating Preston Pearson, our kickoff returner. The fact that he had played for the Steelers the previous year undoubtedly provided extra incentive.

The brilliant Landry knew exactly what the Steelers would do. Bellowing and cursing, a pack of rhinos on the loose in full stride, they charged at Preston. He started to run into the teeth of the charge, then slipped the ball to Hollywood Henderson, who raced up the sidelines for 53 yards before the last player between him and a touchdown, kicker Roy Gerela, managed to get him out of bounds.

It was now you see him, now you don't. I thought the Steelers looked ludicrous, just standing there, watching Henderson chew up yardage in the direction of their goal line. Not that we impressed them—trickery was for sissies. And this play confirmed their opinion of us. Now they figured they'd settle down and beat our brains out.

Did they really think Landry had only one trick up his sleeve? To their total consternation, we scored first, swinging Drew Pearson wide open over the middle to catch a touchdown pass from Roger.

The Steelers came back on the next drive to tie the score at 7, but the game hardly developed into the cake walk they'd expected. Too Tall and I had come of age, and Larry Cole and Jethro Pugh also played the game of their lives. Our *defense* didn't get intimidated. We could handle the Steelers offense, and I could see in their eyes that this fact dawned on them and surprised them.

I can't say our offense made me happy. Golden Richards was flat-out scared. The Steel Curtain intimidated him, and he became null and void as a positive factor. But worse than Golden Richards was tight end Jean Fugett. I believe the Steel Curtain absolutely terrorized him.

This was the Super Bowl, America's most important sporting event, yet Fugett spent much of his time on the bench with an injury I doubted was really serious enough to warrant his sitting out.

I know I played almost the entire Super Bowl hurt. I injured my thigh on the second play of the game but told myself I didn't feel it. Realizing I was playing in the Super Bowl made the thigh feel better, and a few plays later I smashed Franco Harris.

The Steelers rank as the toughest team I've ever seen, before or since. They weren't dirty, but they came close. They broke Golden Richards' ribs and he had to be taken out of the game, but that didn't hurt us because he'd already been thoroughly intimidated.

Jack Lambert kneed Preston Pearson in the groin, right in front of an official, who didn't drop a flag. Lambert also picked up Cliff Harris and dumped him on his head. Again no penalty. Unbelievably, the Steelers, the most physical team ever, didn't draw a penalty the entire game, not even a backfield in motion. Roger Staubach, a man never given to hyperbole, called the officiating "a joke."

Many of our players thought the Steelers intimidated the officials, that the officials feared players like Joe Greene and Ernie Holmes—especially Holmes, who looked as if he could kill you, and probably would, if you looked at him cross-eyed, much less if he saw a penalty being called that hurt his chances to win. But I don't think the Steelers intimidated the officials. They called a bad game, but that was something else. I think so much fierce hitting happened on the field that day that the officials simply decided not to call *anything*. I don't believe a coach or a player, even Ernie Holmes, can intimidate a referee.

How many times *ever* in any big league sport have you seen a player injure an official? I can't remember a single instance. Even an Ernie Holmes knows his career ends, goes kaput, if he hurts a referee. *Fans* intimidate officials. Officials know at any moment that fans, perhaps a whole wave of them, may sweep onto the field as a mob and inflict some serious, even fatal hurt.

Players also fear fans getting out of hand. The angriest I've ever seen a professional athlete get at an official was Joaquin Andujar at umpire Don Denkinger in the 1985 World Series, after Denkinger blew a call at first base in the sixth game of the championship. Yet Andujar never laid a finger on Denkinger. But, to prove my point,

Denkinger received thousands of death threats from fans when the series ended, threats he correctly did not take lightly.

Several Cowboy offensive players thought their offensive line *and the defense* should have fought back against the Steelers. I had no sympathy for this kind of reasoning. Where we, the defense, were concerned, it was our offense's job to deal with what happened to them on the field. We stayed on the sidelines until it was our turn. If Too Tall, Randy, Lee Roy, or I had run onto the field to fight, it would have caused an immediate 15-yard penalty and probably our ejection from the game. Nor should the offensive line have been expected to fight Golden Richards' battles for him. The offensive line had four vicious Steeler All-Pros in their faces all day, more than enough to worry about without also having to worry about the likes of Richards and Fugett.

The half time of Super Bowl X found the score tied 7–7, and into the fourth quarter of this game, which resembled a street fight or a war more than an athletic contest, the Cowboys led 10–7. This is the kind of game we played: Steeler Reggie Harrison blocked one of our punts into the end zone to make the score 10–9 and in the process bit his tongue so hard it was feared he'd lose it.

After the safety we kicked off from our own 20, which gave the Steelers good field position, and they booted a field goal to take a 12–10 lead. The intensity on the field electrified. My own body turned into a mass of hurt, but I kept coming. What else could I do? I could see Too Tall on the other side of the line, just exhausted, a young man but an old warrior, giving everything he had on every play; and Lee Roy behind us, a true root-hog who'd go until he died.

The offense, bless their hearts, threw an interception that gave Pittsburgh the ball on our 7-yard line. But still the Steelers, with all their high-powered guns—Franco Harris, Bradshaw, and Lynn Swann—couldn't put the ball over our goal line. We wouldn't let them. We dug deep inside ourselves, all the way back to places like East Texas State, Tennessee State, and Langston University, and *wouldn't permit* them to make a touchdown. The Steelers settled for a field goal and led 15–10.

Once again our offense failed to move the ball—Mean Joe, Dwight, and Ernie Holmes had also found something extra in themselves. Then came the play that broke our hearts: We charged Bradshaw in an all-out rush, and he got a pass off just a split second before Cliff Harris hammered him in the head, knocking him out of the game. But far down the field Lynn Swann, Super Bowl MVP that day, made a spectacular catch for a 64-yard touchdown. The Steelers led 21–10 with less than three minutes to play.

But Roger had a miracle left. "Never give up the ship" is an old mariner's adage, and this graduate of the Naval Academy certainly never gave up ours. He drove us down the field for a touchdown, the final 38 yards a pass to a former Austin Peay (where do the Cowboys find these schools?) basketball player named Percy Howard.

The Steelers led only 21–17 with 1:48 left to play. The defense dragged itself onto the field for one last stand. Bone-tired, bodies telling us to quit, the will not permitting it, we stopped four straight Steeler runs and gave the ball back to Roger on our own 42-yard line. Just 1:22 remained, with no times out. We'd stopped the clock after each of the Steelers' first three rushes.

Now Mean Joe, Lambert, Mad Dog, and the rest of the Steel Curtain dragged themselves out for *their* last stand.

I stood on the sideline screaming encouragement to Roger and Drew that not even Too Tall, standing next to me, could hear. The noise in the Orange Bowl deafened as the clock ran down to the most dramatic finish in Super Bowl history. Roger ran for 11 yards to midfield as the clock continued to move. He passed to Preston Pearson, a fanatic this entire game, a man consumed by the thought of defeating his former teammates, and we had the ball at the Pittsburgh 38 with twenty-two seconds to go.

I said a "Hail, Mary" for another "Hail, Mary," but the prayer wasn't answered. On the last play of the game, Roger's pass into the end zone was intercepted by Glenn Edwards.

Dwight White sought me out as I trudged off the field. He put his arms around me, big brother to little brother, and said, "You fought hard."

I didn't talk to anyone in the locker room. I sank to a low I'd never known before. To get so close, to savor and inhale the sweet smell of victory and then come away with nothing was the worst feeling I'd ever known.

One of the hardest things I've ever had to do occurred shortly after the game when I broadcast my last radio show of the season for KRLD. All I could think to do was apologize sincerely to the Dallas fans for not winning, but I told them truthfully we'd done our best. "I promise you," I concluded, "we'll be back in the Super Bowl."

That night, mostly for the sake of Mom, Dad, Sharon, and my sister, Mary, I attended the Super Bowl party Cowboys owner Clint Murchison threw for the team.

I had made quite an impression the first time I met the billionaire Cowboys owner, although hardly a favorable one. It was 1973, my rookie year, and I had waited, super-eager, to get put in the game. When the word finally came to go on the field, I charged forward and in my zeal ran over a little guy standing on the sideline. "Can't we keep dudes with no business here away from us?" I snarled over my shoulder.

The dude "with no business here" whom I'd flattened was none other than Clint Murchison, the man who signed my paychecks.

Willie Nelson entertained at the Super Bowl party and appeared as morose as any player. Thomas Henderson, who dated one of the Pointer Sisters, Alice, brought her to the gathering. She seemed a very nice person, but Thomas kept shaking his head. "I don't think she's pretty enough for me to date," he whispered in my unbelieving ear.

Once I put the season in perspective, I realized how much we'd accomplished. A team of "babies," we'd succeeded because of Landry's great coaching. He even loosened up on rules, which I don't think he'd ever done before, and I know he didn't do it after that. We had had no curfew that season, which went against Landry's instincts. But he had seen something in us and decided to gamble, and it worked. We had a tremendous *self*-discipline, the best form of discipline. Coaches can try to fire up a player, but if a flame doesn't burn from inside, all the exhortations in the world won't do any good. The 1975 Cowboys disciplined themselves and, on the rare occasions it was needed, one another. Quiet talk by a veteran with a partying rookie always managed to keep the rookie on the straight and narrow.

In 1975 I fully came to realize what a great coach we had. I understood what Gary Cartwright once wrote: "There are those in football, Giants' president Wellington Mara among them, who feel that Tom Landry has perfected, maybe even invented, football's modern defense."

"Landry used to be ultra-frustrating," said my friend Don Meredith. "I thought I knew a little about football. But Landry would be up at the blackboard saying, 'Okay, we'll do this . . . then they'll do that . . . then we'll . . .' You'd interrupt him and say, 'Coach, what if they *don't* do that?' Landry would just look at you and say, 'They will.' "

It's true. Landry would tell us what to expect, and perhaps ninety percent of the time, a phenomenal average, he'd be right. Of course, knowing what our opponent would do next provided us a big advantage.

Tom Landry played a major role in my life. Many people joke that he was born into the job of Dallas

Cowboys coach, but actually his earlier history is very interesting. He started as quarterback for the University of Texas, broke his thumb, and got replaced by future Hall-of-Famer Bobby Layne. But Landry didn't let the broken thumb keep him out of the lineup. He started the next game at fullback and rushed for more than 100 yards against a North Carolina squad that featured Charlie "Choo Choo" Justice, a legendary back of the 1940s.

Landry spent six years at cornerback for the New York Giants, the last four of these serving double duty as an assistant coach. Once, when all the New York quarterbacks were injured, Landry took over at the position. He played fifty-nine minutes in the game, switching to the defensive backfield when the Giants didn't have the ball.

In the late 1950s the Giants defense was Assistant Coach Landry's responsibility; Vince Lombardi handled the offense. The two provided quite a contrast: Lombardi, emotional, high strung, screamed at everybody; Landry, the football scholar, never raised his voice.

Lombardi took over the Green Bay Packers in 1959, the year before Clint Murchison hired Landry to head the expansion Cowboys franchise. Not surprisingly, Dallas became the first expansion team to achieve championship status.

Landry's first love may have been defense, but he also did master work on offense. "Landry created great defense," Gary Cartwright wrote, "then began experimenting with offenses that would destroy it." The result: the most sophisticated, Space Age, state-of-the-art attack in football. The movement of our offense, much of it invisible to the casual fan, kept defenses constantly off balance. Our offense had to be good because Landry designed offenses he thought capable of defeating his own superb defense.

I've wondered about this. Landry is a quiet, calm, almost stoical man. He never boasts. He shoulders defeats with the same grace as victories. I doubt if he would talk much about designing offenses to stop his own defense, making me wonder if deep in his heart the defenses of other teams didn't provide challenge enough for this brilliant tactician. Would only his own defense suffice? Was going against himself the most rewarding competition?

Landry never gave a fiery locker room talk, not even before the start of Super Bowl X. All he said was, "We've done all we can do in preparation. This is the biggest game in our business."

For Landry, that was an emotional speech—mentioning the importance of the game. He usually didn't do that. Certainly our preparation for Super Bowl X had been no different from getting ready for, say, the lowly Detroit Lions. The routines didn't vary. The emphasis was always on *execution,* doing things right. We knew *we'd* be the ones to lose the game. There'd be no blaming it on the coach.

And we didn't. We knew we probably would not have come within an eyelash of beating the Steelers had it not been for Landry. The best part, as we looked forward to the 1976 season: We were a young powerhouse team that had not yet reached its peak.

Taking a break from filming a Big Brothers commercial

Here I am with some young players.

Getting to Gifford Nielson of the Oilers.

Overleaf:

Too Tall and I give Clint Longley a headache. He'd gone to the San Diego Chargers after his fight with Roger Staubach.

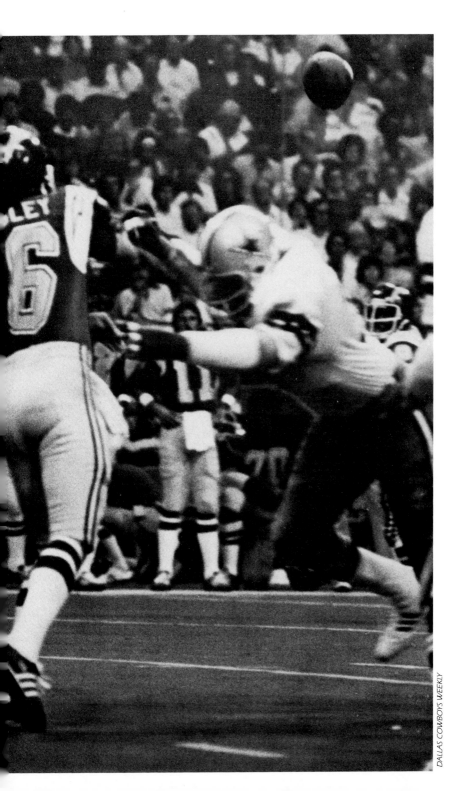

Too Tall and I are sacking Bob Avellini of the Bears.

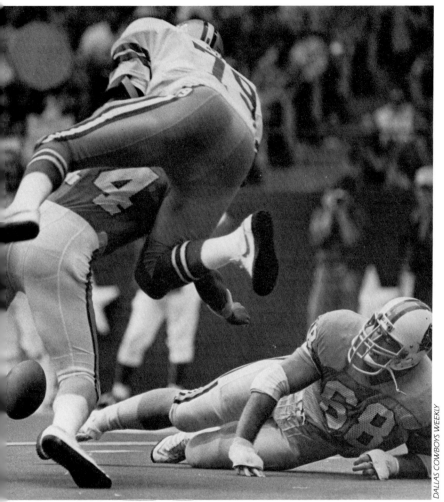

Forcing Gifford Nielson to fumble

**Carrying the funeral wreath
to the Redskins' dressing room**

7

The first time I realized my life had changed drastically came in February 1976, a few weeks after the Super Bowl. I took a date to a movie, and the crowd waiting in line to buy tickets wound around the theater. Previously I'd developed a trick for avoiding these lines by asking for the manager and telling him I took water pills and needed to urinate often. This was true enough, the result of a weight control program I maintained, and the manager invariably let my date and me in ahead of the others. This night when I encountered the manager, his face lit up as if he'd met happiness itself. "Come right in, Mr. Martin," he gushed. "Come in free."

I insisted on paying. I never felt comfortable with people picking up my tabs, although there were many offers.

Appearing in the Super Bowl made every Cowboy a hero in Dallas, and it became virtually impossible to step onto the street without being patted on the back and asked for an autograph. Heavy stuff, and some of it went to my head.

About this time Dr. Pepper hired me to start a Young Cowboys program, joining Jim Sundberg, of the Texas Rangers' Junior Rangers program, and Ken Cooper, with his Young Tornadoes soccer program. Children were urged to become Young Cowboys, and I received literally thousands of letters, all of which I tried personally to answer. It wasn't possible. But hardly a day went by that I didn't meet and talk to groups of kids. Thus began a considerable relationship with Dr. Pepper, which soon became one of the sponsors of my radio show.

I did take a one-week vacation, flying to Pittsburgh at Dwight White's invitation, so I could ride back to Dallas with him, where he intended to visit his parents. Dwight let me drive his Mercedes, purchased with his share of the winning Super Bowl purse. I remember we stayed overnight at singer Roger Miller's King of the Road Motel in Tennessee. The front desk featured a ceramic statue of a black kid sitting on a watermelon rind. I looked at Dwight, wondering if he'd want to tear up the motel, as he'd once wanted to tear up that Louisiana bar. Although fire burned in his eyes, he shrugged it off.

This off-season I got heavy into the party scene. I went regularly to various Dallas nightclubs with Too Tall and Thomas Henderson. Thomas had just moved into Too Tall's house. The only thing they shared was an appreciation of beautiful women. I didn't yet know it, but Henderson had long been heavy into drugs, maintaining a colossal habit that at times cost him more than $2,000 a week.

Too Tall, on the other hand, used no drugs, drank only beer—he held the Cowboy beer-drinking championship—and he, too, remained in the dark about Henderson's growing addiction.

The three of us would visit a nightclub and pick up four or five girls. (Actually, we wouldn't have to pick them up; they'd join us at our table.) Then we'd take the girls to another nightclub, collect four or five more, and go to still another club. A few friends usually accompanied us, and they'd bring girls over to our table as well. These friends figured whatever was left over, still spectacular, would go to them. Four or five nightclubs later, the girls, Thomas, Too Tall, myself, and the friends would return to Too Tall's house for what could only be called a wild party.

Henderson, whom Too Tall ultimately threw out of his home, once sneaked *five* women into the training camp dorm at Thousand Oaks. He dated a Cowboy cheerleader, a rich Highland Park matron, a Playboy Bunny. He went with college graduates and street people. "Sometimes I didn't even take my shoes off," he said.

At Too Tall's house there were usually five or six beautiful women to every guy. Henderson, a tremendous stud in the sex department, came in a distant second to Too Tall. Too Tall was insatiable. He'd go from room to room servicing the girls. When he ran out of rooms, there was always the pool table or the floor. No Arabian sheik ever had such a tempting harem. And there were different girls every night. All we needed to do was make the nightclub rounds.

My activities started to strain my relationship with the liberated Sharon Bell, and she knew only the tip of the iceberg. But, fresh from the titanic battle with the Steelers, I thought myself the big-shot Cowboy and enjoyed myself too much to stop the playing. Certainly I behaved the opposite of what might have been expected from the childhood my mother gave me.

I did become more selective. I continued to make my club rounds with Thomas and Too Tall, but when we got back to Too Tall's, I'd zero in on the most beautiful girl, and take her to the apartment I'd recently rented. This irritated Too Tall; he didn't want even one less girl in his house.

Later Henderson wrote of these times in *Playboy:*

But I never could keep up with Too Tall. Many nights when I was played out, asleep next to some chick, he would come into my room and tap me on my foot, "You mind if I get me some?"

On Too Tall's birthday one year, I gave him a blonde, a redhead, and a brunette. When he came home, they were all spread out for him. I admit I shared his birthday present with him.

*   *   *

Doomsday II, the name of our great defense, came into being after the 1975 Super Bowl.

Gil Brandt and his computers made valuable additions to our squad for the 1976 season: kicker Efren Herrera, quarterback Danny White, defensive back Aaron Kyle, and wide receiver Butch Johnson.

Butch impressed me right away. His dad came with him to the first training camp, which I thought a wonderful gesture, a great show of support. Butch lived near Thousand Oaks and often he'd bring me a plate of chitlins back from his home. He was an aggressive rookie who'd caught more than sixty passes his senior year in college, despite being hurt much of the season. If Butch got his hands near a ball, he caught it.

We also added offensive lineman Tom Rafferty from Penn State and tight end Jay Saldi from South Carolina, both of whom came to play important roles in our future. A player we *lost* made me just as happy: Jean Fugett got a fat contract and went to the Redskins. They could have him.

We were favored to repeat in 1976 and go to the Super Bowl and play the Steelers once again. Our defense remained as good as any that existed, with Too Tall, myself, Randy White, Thomas Henderson, and the rest. We had potent weapons on offense, especially with Roger throwing to Drew. I thought us solid but unspectacular at the running back positions. Landry intended to alternate the running back combination of Robert Newhouse and Preston Pearson with the team of Charles Young and Doug Dennison.

We won our first eight games of the season! I got a slow start in the sack department, garnering only one in the first five games, but by season's end I again led the team with fifteen. In the early games I came too fast. The quarterback stepped up into the pocket, and I'd simply miss, fly right by him. Nevertheless, much of my job got accomplished purely by getting close to the quarterback and altering his rhythm. A rattled quarterback can hurt his team. Quarterbacks I learned we could rattle included Joe Theisman, Jim Hart, Ron Jaworski, Steve Bartkowski, and, I'm sorry to say, Fran Tarkenton. Tarkenton once called me "the best pass rusher of all time," extremely high praise coming from a Hall-of-Famer.

Quarterbacks who couldn't be shaken, no matter how roughly you handled them, were Joe Montana, Terry Bradshaw, Ken Stabler, Dan Fouts, and Doug Williams.

The difference between the rattled quarterback and the imperturbable quarterback is that the former can be frightened into throwing the ball before he has a receiver open, and that leads to killing interceptions.

The Cowboys had a major rivalry with the St. Louis Cardinals. The Cardinals' lightning-quick receiver Mel Gray always seemed to burn us on long touchdown receptions. Each time he caught a touchdown pass against us, he wheeled around and spiked the ball in the end zone, which I felt embarrassed our defensive backs.

Nineteen seventy-six was no different. He caught a long touchdown pass against us, but this time there was a difference. When I saw him catch the pass, I ran down the field after him and, as he wheeled to spike the ball, pointed my finger straight into his face. "You spike the ball," I growled, "and I'll break your fucking nose again." Gray looked at me and decided not to spike the ball. His nose had been broken three weeks before against Green Bay, and he figured I meant what I said.

We finished our 1976 season with an 11–3 record, a game better than the 10–4 we'd established in our 1975 Super Bowl year. The trouble was, we lost the last game of the regular season 27–14 to Washington, which meant we entered the playoffs on a down note.

A Landry rule-of thumb: Once you're assured of making the playoffs, you must make certain never to lose

another game. Football is a sport of momentum and the
great teams never slacken pace as the championship ap-
proaches.

Most of our running backs suffered from injuries heading into the playoffs, and Roger had had a hard time with
certain of his receivers. In the sixth-from-last game of the
season, Charlie Young dropped two touchdown passes in
a 27–14 loss to the Cardinals. Landry never let him off the
bench again. That was Landry's way: If you didn't pro-
duce, you didn't play. Landry then tried to make Beasley
Reese, who had the speed of the gods, into a pass receiver, but Reese, as they say, couldn't catch a cold.

Before the playoff game against the Los Angeles
Rams, I saw Ernie Stautner approaching with a big grin on
his face. "What are you smiling about, Ernie?" I asked.

"You've just been voted into the Pro Bowl," he said.

I knew I'd won quite an honor, even more meaningful
since it is the other NFL players who vote people into the
Pro Bowl—high recognition from my peers. But as I later
learned, what's given can also be taken away. I'd be an
All-Pro choice later but wouldn't get voted into the Pro
Bowl. Too many players came to resent my all-out, free-
wheeling style of play on every down.

Other Cowboys voted into the Pro Bowl in 1976 were
Billy Joe DuPree, Drew Pearson, Cliff Harris, Rayfield
Wright, and Roger Staubach.

We held the Rams to just 14 points in the divisional
playoff, but Roger and company could manage only 12.
We simply had no running game, and being forced into
passing on every down rendered Roger less effective.

One player, I moaned to myself, just one running back,
and we'd be the best damn team God ever gave breath to.

I enjoyed the Pro Bowl, played in Seattle, an expansion city. However, we practiced in San Diego. Practice
consisted of absolutely no hitting and a lot of partying.
The young women of San Diego proved every bit as
willing as those in Dallas. I had a ball.

The next three Pro Bowls had already been scheduled for Tampa, Los Angeles, and Hawaii, and I vowed I'd play in all three. I didn't break my promise.

Bob Lilly became an amateur photographer, and I decided this off-season was a good time for me to take up the hobby. I paid for good lessons and good equipment, and even sold some pictures. But instead of shooting Roger Staubach wrapped in a towel, I thought, why not take photos of pretty girls? I contacted Suzanne Mitchell, head of the Dallas Cowboy Cheerleaders, and got her permission to photograph the cheerleader tryouts.

I didn't know much. What I wanted most was to see the girls. Real photographers, there in droves, gave me tips on what to shoot—and got a good laugh when they found out I was using the wrong type of lens.

I went to see the girls, but really didn't like what I saw. One cheerleader not elected back on the team let out a terrible scream when she heard the news, then cried and ran around in circles. She looked so pitiful and forlorn. The cheerleader tryouts reminded me exactly of the tryouts for the Cowboy football team: cutthroat.

Tex Schramm told the cheerleaders they couldn't date or even *talk* to the players. The key to the situation was that he gave the order to the cheerleaders, *not* the players. The girls were pretty certain to obey because they had a threat hanging over their heads. Besides, it's a lot easier to talk tough to a 98-pound female than to a 280-pound lineman.

I dated cheerleaders anyway, and so did Thomas Henderson, Too Tall Jones, Golden Richards, and Jay Saldi.

This off-season I worked super-hard, not only at being in shape for the 1977 schedule, but also full-time for Dr. Pepper. The company gave me an office and desk, and I decided to learn the business from the ground up. I rode on Dr. Pepper trucks for a week to learn the business and became friends with many drivers. I lifted cases, carrying them in and out of stores, and served in every way as assistant to the driver. The first driver I rode with spread the word about me. One day he asked me to toss a case of soda on top of a truck. I underestimated my strength and threw it all the way over to the other side, where it crashed on the ground. "Maybe you've been lifting too many weights," the driver observed with amusement.

Dr. Pepper assigned me to find out why the soft drink enjoyed a 25 percent increase in sales in affluent North Dallas at the same time that it showed a 1.6 percent decrease in minority areas. I already knew why, but, before informing my bosses, dutifully went about the job of compiling research anyway.

Minorities prefer fruit flavors—orange, grape, strawberry; they always have. I also photographed shelf space showing Dr. Pepper's six-ounce fruit-flavored Salute drink next to sixteen-ounce bottles the competition sold for only a few cents more. As a youngster, I myself would have bought from the competition, watching out for pennies.

I suggested to Dr. Pepper management that they bring Orange Crush to Dallas—buy the formula and market it in the city. Orange Crush already had major name identification. By following my suggestions, Dr. Pepper immediately made an impact in minority areas.

I also discovered that Dr. Pepper didn't have a single major hotel account for their soft drinks. I went to the Hyatt Regency, then under construction, wearing a hard hat and remembering from my college days that the soft drink machines at East Texas State bore the school's logo, not the corporation's. After a talk with the Hyatt Regency management, I went to my bosses at Dr. Pepper and suggested they *give* machines to the hotel chain and, instead of Dr. Pepper advertising, put the hotel directory on the machine. Dr. Pepper agreed, and soon they had the major hotel account they'd been looking for. I also talked the Cowboys into replacing Coke with Dr. Pepper at our training center, which lent Dr. Pepper considerable prestige.

Meanwhile I continued to work out religiously at the Cowboy training center. While pumping iron there I learned that we had made what became a rather famous deal giving us the first-round draft pick of the Seattle Seahawks: the First of the First. It meant, in effect, that the Cowboys would get University of Pittsburgh star running back Tony Dorsett, the most ballyhooed star to enter the NFL since O. J. Simpson.

"We're going to the Super Bowl!" I yelled that day at the training center to anyone who would listen. "We're going to the Super Bowl again!"

Tony Dorsett impressed me immediately. He spoke well, handled himself like a gentleman, and at that time certainly used no drugs. Tony moved into the apartment complex where I lived, and I joked with him about his car, a giant Lincoln Continental, which I called "a land yacht."

I studied Dorsett closely, knowing we needed a breakaway back, praying that, as advertised, he really held the answer to our main shortcoming.

Dorsett turned out to be even more talented than anyone expected. It was almost this simple: If a defensive man missed him, Dorsett scored.

The Cowboys had loaded themselves for bear in 1977. Tony "Thrill" Hill became a rookie pass-catching sensation, and Landry finally decided to move Randy White permanently onto the defensive line. With Too Tall, Jethro Pugh, Randy White, and myself on the defensive line, I thought we fielded a front four second to none. The tenacious, scrappy Lee Roy Jordan retired from the linebacking corps, but we still had Bob Breunig, D. D. Lewis, and the enormously gifted Hollywood Henderson. The defensive backfield featured Cliff Harris, Charlie Waters, Benny Barnes, and Mark Washington.

Our defense could stop anybody.

In 1977, league statistics (which don't lie—or do they?) showed us to be the Number One rated defense in the entire NFL.

And even I admired the offense. We had two high-powered future Hall-of-Famers, Roger and Drew, to fuel the passing game; the flashy rookie Tony Hill to take pressure off Drew; an outstanding tight end in Billy Joe DuPree; and a solid offensive line anchored by Rayfield Wright and Ralph Neely. We owned the most reliable back in the NFL, Preston Pearson, plus fireplug fullback Robert Newhouse—and, of course, future superstar Tony Dorsett waiting in the wings.

In 1977, league statistics also showed us to be the Number One rated offense in the entire NFL.

Besides having the best offense and defense in all the world of football, we had something intangible but perhaps even more important: This team was obsessed with winning. Everybody talked about winning, expected to win, played to win, and accepted nothing else.

I had two personal goals: make the Pro Bowl and win the Super Bowl.

Coach Landry, who had unexpectedly loosened up the rules in 1975, when we had our dirty dozen rookies, decided to tighten ship. Curfews again ruled the night, and players had to wear jackets and ties on road trips.

I don't know why Landry reverted to his old self. I did what he ordered, but I couldn't figure out what difference what you wore in your off hours made on the football field. A lot of guys griped—they'd bought flashy clothes to wear on trips—but I thought it a tempest in a teapot. Players will always gripe.

On weeknights—especially Thursday and Friday—Too Tall, Hollywood, and I continued to make the rounds of Dallas nightclubs, always ending up at Too Tall's house with some of the most beautiful women in the city. Other players, black and white alike, began stopping by to get in on the action. Too Tall is slow to anger, but I could tell he grew hot about my zeroing in each night on the best-looking woman and then splitting to my place with her. On the field an opponent could try on every play to reek mayhem on Too Tall—legal and illegal—and he'd keep his cool. Off the field I could burn him by splitting with one of the women.

Most times the girls would change into a T-shirt, nothing more (a Cowboy T-shirt, of course), then the fun would begin. Rome in the days of Caesar was never so sweet.

My reputation as a diligent student of game films led me to provide the alibi several married Cowboys used when they wanted to go to Too Tall's. "Got to study films with Harvey," they'd tell their wives.

Women, seemingly an unending number of them, were always available to Cowboy football players, especially the stars. The temptation was terrific, and only a few hardy souls, like Roger, consistently resisted. That was simply how Staubach was.

Craig Morton once sneaked a pair of lovelies into the team dorm, only to be disappointed when he learned that what they really wanted was Roger Staubach's autograph. Why not? thought Morton. He took them into Staubach's room, where the star quarterback lay sleeping, wearing only his undershorts. When Staubach awakened, his face turned red. "Would you like to see pictures of my wife and kids?" he managed to stammer.

Thomas Henderson thought Roger a square—an old fashioned stick-in-the-mud, a have-no-fun straight arrow whom we had to tolerate because he won football games. On Thomas's list of priorities this ranked somewhere below sex and drugs. Future events proved Roger's course the wiser one. Today he's an eminently successful Dallas businessman; Thomas Henderson is in prison.

After the 1977 season, Sharon Bell rightly got fed up with my womanizing and moved back to San Francisco to be near her parents. She left the impression that if I ever decided to settle down—"grow up," she put it, there might be a future for us. I hated to see her go, but not enough to stop her. We kept in touch via long distance phone and on trips I made to the West Coast.

About this time I bought a beautiful house in Carrollton, a North Dallas suburb. I still live in the house and own it. It has an indoor swimming pool, fireplace, and four bedrooms.

If Cowboy players cheated on their girl friends and wives, it worked the other way as well. The density of some players amazed me. They'd bring their wives to a nightclub, disappear with the first good-looking woman they saw, and leave their wives and girl friends to fend for themselves. They often managed quite nicely. There was always an ample supply of men to step in and take them out or to bed while hubby played on his own.

Still, the players were much more sexually active than their wives. Maybe because of the milieu we hung out in, women were almost always available. Older, wealthy, bored Highland Park women (Highland Park may be the richest community in the United States) married to bankers, oil men, or business executives—the movers and shakers of Dallas—vied with younger women to be part of the action we provided.

I found time for everything, including sleep and football. My salary stood at only $45,000 a year, but I took down $20,000 from Dr. Pepper, $15,000 from KRLD, and much more from personal appearances: *Sports Illustrated* called me "Dallas's highest profile Cowboy." I began doing commercials for Mercantile Bank, and was dumbfounded the first time I walked into the place. My picture had been hung all over the bank.

I believed I worked and played so hard, set such a frenetic pace, because I feared time would soon run out for me. I'd just reached my peak as a football player, but how many years could I realistically expect to play? My career might end in an instant with an exploded knee, or even with me paralyzed, as tragically happened with Darryl Stingley of New England. That my time would come to an end I couldn't doubt. Each year players, friends I'd thought somehow would be around forever, turned up missing. Besides Lee Roy Jordan that year, Dave Edwards also retired. Stories were legend of veterans leaving the NFL after ten or more years to face lives of loneliness and desperation. I knew I needed to be prepared for life after football.

My investment in Balls, which had looked so bright in the beginning, wound up costing me money when it closed.

In the spring of 1977 I ate at a barbecue restaurant called Smokey John's. The food was terrific, but the place stood nearly empty. I talked to John himself and told him I'd like to buy into the restaurant. "You keep the food like it is," I said, "and I'll bring the people in."

With a one-third ownership in the barbecue ribs restaurant, I set about with my usual gusto to attract customers. Soon Smokey John's did a brisk business.

Also that spring I served for one week as sports anchorman for Channel 4, the CBS affiliate in Dallas. This provided the dual benefits of gaining experience on TV and being able to see myself as others did. I had talent as a speaker, but my looks could only be called problematic.

It was an old problem, my deformed jaw. Sharon Bell, who had not yet gone to San Francisco, recommended a good orthodontist. I went to him and he put braces on my teeth and planned reconstructive surgery once the 1977 season had ended.

I organized a charity basketball game between players from the Steelers and Cowboys, the opponents in Super Bowl X. The Cowboys slaughtered the Steelers in this game—scant consolation for our defeat for the world championship.

Actually, the Steelers never had a chance. On our team

were former college stars Percy Howard, who'd been a
teammate of Fly Williams, and former Big Ten sensation
Preston Pearson, who numbered among his many basketball accomplishments blocking a shot by Kareem Abdul-
Jabbar (an incident Preston never tired of talking about).
Percy, who caught that touchdown pass in Super Bowl X,
and Preston, who caught three touchdown passes in the
NFC championship game against the Rams, never played
a down of college football. Score two more points for
those Cowboy computers and the brilliance of Tom Landry and Gil Brandt for recognizing diamonds in the rough.

I'd given Gene Jacobson, an accountant and friend of
mine, a lot of authority when it came to handling my
money. Gene liked to be around football players, especially the well-known ones. He advised me against invest-
ing in Smokey John's, but I did that anyway. He did
advise that I invest in a restaurant called Recipe's on
Greenville Avenue and Park Lane, and I took the plunge.

Recipe's catered to a high-dollar Highland Park clien-
tele. Gene managed to hire one of the finest chefs in Dallas
away from the Fairmont Hotel, and I liked a gimmick he
introduced: giving printed copies of the recipes we used to
any customer who wanted them.

As I headed for 1977 training camp at Thousand Oaks,
I thought my future looked bright—even if, God forbid, I
suffered some career-ending injury. I figured my fledgling
investments, coupled with my enormous energy, would
see me through anything.

That year at training camp I kept a diary, and it is eye-
opening reading now. I've heard the mind blots out what
is unpleasant, but fortunately my diary won't allow me to
do that. "I feel like hell," read one day's entry. "Lots of
grass drills tomorrow. Oh my God," read another. On a
third day: "I think I'm gonna die."

And I was a veteran! I knew what to expect from

Landry. I suppose I would have felt sorry for rookies who didn't know what to expect, if feeling sorry for rookies comprised even the slightest part of a veteran's makeup. But it didn't. Veterans rooted for veterans, friends who'd been tested together on the field, especially in that awesome war of Super Bowl X.

All eyes, including my own, focused on Tony Dorsett, who promptly got injured. Not to worry, I thought, at least not now. Preston Pearson, always reliable, suddenly became absolutely brilliant. He rose beyond himself, became better than he was—a player who couldn't conceivably perform this well, but did. Preston started in place of Tony Dorsett, but all of us knew it was only a matter of time before the change came. We compared Preston to a dependable never-let-you-down Volkswagen Rabbit, Tony Dorsett to a sleek Mercedes. Also, we knew the Cowboys hadn't given away a multitude of talent to have Dorsett sit on the bench. No matter what Preston did—and he played spectacularly—he'd be replaced.

We won our first eight games of the season, then lost a tough one to St. Louis 24–17. The timing of Dorsett's replacement of Preston Pearson couldn't have been worse. It came after our first loss of the season, a game in which Preston, if not the team, played particularly well. But any timing would have been bad when replacing a respected, high-performance veteran with a rookie.

Preston could have raised a fuss but, like a true pro, kept his bitterness to himself. Like everyone else on the team, he knew Tony Dorsett could go from Point A to Point B faster than anyone in the world. Preston adjusted to a new role, and became the best clutch third-down pass receiver in the NFL.

We should have gone undefeated that year. We lost to the Cardinals because they got sky high for us, while we had an off-day. We lost only one other game, 28–13, to the Steelers in Pittsburgh. We made a lot of mistakes, which you can't do against Pittsburgh. This loss hurt us personally, but it was a reminder that football, unlike boxing, is a team sport, not an individual one. Muhammad Ali at his peak would never lose a fight, but a team is not made up of forty-five Muhammad Alis all working in perfect synchronization. A bad day by even the least member of a football team can mean defeat.

I talked to Dwight White over the phone several days after the Steelers game, and what he told me got me boiling mad. He said most of the Steelers still viewed us as sissies. They didn't believe we possessed the toughness needed to win a Super Bowl.

I knew the Steelers were full of crap.

Personally, I consider 1977 my greatest year. I recorded twenty-three sacks in the first eleven games and terrorized quarterbacks so much that the next year the league included sacks as an official part of its records. Bubba Baker tied my record of twenty-three sacks, but no one has ever beaten it. And consider that my twenty-three sacks came in just a fourteen-game season, not the current format of sixteen.

I got elected to the Pro Bowl when the 1977 season ended. I also was a *unanimous* choice for All-Pro, and got named Defensive MVP in the NFL. A still higher honor awaited, at least in the minds of sportswriters.

But the highest honor I received—and the world already seemed like paradise—came during a team meeting before the season even began. Coach Landry announced I would be the captain of his beloved Flex defense. "Harvey deserves it," was the only explanation he thought necessary.

I took the job of captain seriously. I became a screamer, as Lee Roy Jordan had been (although no one could be as loud as Lee Roy), and never tired of speaking to teammates if I thought the slightest chance existed they'd let up.

We defeated Denver 14–6 in the final game of the regular season, thus heading ourselves into the playoffs on

a positive note. We smashed the Bears 37–7 in the divisional playoff, and then trounced Minnesota 23–6 in the
NFC championship game.

The oddsmakers tabbed us a 5-point favorite to defeat
the Denver Broncos in Super Bowl XII, which I thought a
joke. I *knew* we'd kill them.

For days before the opening kickoff, I concentrated on
Andy Maurer. Maurer, the offensive tackle I'd be matched
against, was short, big, strong, and slow. The key part
was slow. I could do the 40 in 4:7, and I didn't think the
offensive lineman existed whom I couldn't outquick. And
although I didn't need any extra incentive, I had it playing
in another Super Bowl. In the last game of the regular
season against these same Broncos, I had *no* sacks, a fact
Andy Maurer boasted about when the press asked what he
thought of me. *No sacks, huh?* I thought. *When I get my
hands on you again, I'll mop the field with your ass.*

I spent most of Super Bowl week feeling totally confi-
dent, nearly going blind watching game films with Randy
White. Randy would be matched against Bronco left guard
Tom Glassic, who didn't have the strength to handle
White. (But no one really had the strength to deal with
him. Opponents routinely double- and even triple-teamed
Randy.)

I believe the supreme confidence we felt was completely justified and thoroughly healthy. We'd played the
Broncos during the regular season at three-quarter speed
(granted, their starting quarterback, Craig Morton,
missed the game) and still beat them, and a clear-eyed
examination of our two rosters made it plain who had the
better players.

Our confidence was of the healthiest kind. A superior
team should not waste time building an opponent into
some imaginary Titan. We had better personnel than
Denver and intended to prove it.

I'd been in great physical condition the entire year, and
so had the other Cowboys. Beneath a cool, almost gla-

cierlike exterior, a trademark of our team, we possessed the highest, most intense motivation, and it came from within.

Players didn't miss curfews to sample New Orleans' flavorful French Quarter cuisine. Each of us resolved to stick to business, figuring postgame *victory* celebrations would be much sweeter. Also, most of us remembered too vividly the terrible, mind-destroying depression that haunted us after our 21–17 Super Bowl X loss to the Steelers. Working hard to avoid a repeat of that hellish experience got us ready for Denver.

I played mother hen. I wanted to make sure everyone kept his head on straight, and called three or four defensive team meetings, none of which probably affected the outcome of the game. I kept emphasizing that all good things happen to a winner. As Cowboys, with all the attention we received, sometimes we forgot the one reason for all the attention—"because Cowboys win."

I couldn't fill my days full enough. Hundreds of photographers swarmed everywhere, and I made myself the most available Cowboy. Ego didn't apply here. I got paid every time my picture was taken with me wearing a Mercantile Bank T-shirt, and I'd brought along an adequate supply.

About five days before the Super Bowl game I almost relived an embarrassment from my rookie year. That year I had a girl in my room one night when offensive line coach Jim Myers came around checking for curfew violations. I managed to get her in the bathroom before he got inside the door and suspiciously looked around.

"You got anything in here?" he asked.

"No."

Just then the toilet flushed.

At the team meeting the next day I heard Landry intone, "Rookie violated rules. It was Martin. Three hundred dollars."

Now as a veteran, I once again had a young woman in

my room, and again Coach Myers came to check. I was supposed to be alone, and he'd become suspicious upon noticing I'd ordered two meals from room service. This time he didn't discover the girl in the bathroom. I convinced him I felt ravenous hunger, although the opposite was true. I got myself so keyed up for the Super Bowl that I had no appetite for food.

When I didn't concentrate on Andy Maurer on Super Bowl XII week, I entertained myself with thoughts of what Too Tall would do to Bronco offensive tackle Claudie Minor. A total mismatch. But then, just about anybody against Too Tall is a mismatch.

I played outside of Randy at right end, both of us designated All-Pro. I don't know of another instance when two players on the same side of a defensive line won that honor the same year.

The Cowboy front four didn't have to worry about what would happen in the unlikely event a Bronco got beyond us. Hollywood Henderson had more raw talent than any linebacker living. He possessed talents superior even to the current prototype, Lawrence Taylor. But Henderson's problem was that he knew it. He felt people owed him something simply because he had such talent. Thomas, Too Tall, and I were very close off the field, and by now I realized he had problems. I tried to help, as so many others did later, but no one could save Hollywood from himself.

As of Super Bowl XII, however, Henderson's personal demons had not yet mushroomed large enough to diminish his performance. His awesome skills could withstand a great deal before they slipped away from him.

Henderson once smashed into Minnesota Viking punt returner Manfred Moore so violently that *Dallas Morning News* reporter Bob St. John wrote, "Moore appeared to be dead."

Henderson, for him, stayed straight when it came time for the Super Bowl XII game. The same can't be said for what happened two days *after*. He rented a limo, bought some cocaine, and drove to Los Angeles to stay at the Beverly Wilshire Hotel. There he met people like the Temptations and Richard Pryor and used a gram a day of cocaine for the two weeks he spent in Tinseltown.

Cowboy linebacker D. D. Lewis guaranteed more grief to the Broncos in Super Bowl XII. "Only" six feet two inches and 220 pounds, D.D. was the toughest "little man" I knew—smart, always in the right place, a fierce competitor. D.D. correctly judged that Henderson didn't work hard enough and constantly got right in Hollywood's face to argue with him, scream at him, anything.

Of course, the Cowboys had the Broncos outcoached by a big margin. This doesn't demean in any way the ability of Denver's Red Miller. Landry outcoaches everybody.

When we came onto the Superdome field the noise was unbelievable, threatening to burst eardrums. If we didn't adjust, I thought, somehow orient ourselves, the sound could prove a bigger menace than the Broncos. Worse, I believed Denver had more rooters there than we did. The dominant color in the stands was orange. No one should underestimate the impact of a crowd on the performance of a team.

Nevertheless, I knew "home crowd" advantage probably wouldn't mean anything in this game. A crowd can pump a sagging team up, lift it sky high, exhort it to perform at 100 percent of ability. But in a Super Bowl or a championship in any other sport, the players are already completely motivated. There is nothing more for a crowd to extract from them.

The captains met at the center of the field for the coin flip. Craig Morton, a former quarterback of the Cowboys who ended up with Denver, represented the Bronco offense. (Morton went to the Giants and then Denver after Landry decided to go full-time with Roger Staubach as quarterback.)

I knew Craig had a lot of ability. If Roger beat him in the talent department, it wasn't by much. I liked the way Craig dressed off the field, too. He reminded me of someone just photographed for *Gentleman's Quarterly*.

I figured Craig Morton knew the relative strengths of the two teams better than any other player, since he'd quarterbacked both. I looked into his eyes as we shook hands in the center of the field. He quickly glanced away, in my opinion a certain giveaway that his analysis of the coming game coincided with mine. I saw fear in Morton's eyes as I glared at him. He knew I was no longer the timid rookie he'd known in 1973.

"Morton's scared," I told Too Tall when I got back to the sidelines.

"Oughta be," said Jones.

We won the coin toss and elected to receive. I had hoped we'd choose to kick off so we could get right to the task of beating heads.

On the first scrimmage play, Landry called a double reverse, and Butch Johnson fumbled the ball, recovering it himself but losing 20 yards. I pawed the Astroturf on the sidelines, telling myself we didn't need the offense.

The call on the first play typified Landry. Most coaches become conservative in a big game. They fear looking bad, and they play *not to lose*. Landry plays to win.

The Bronco offense started their first series with good field position close to midfield. We took our defensive positions amid noise that simply deafened. The Bronco fans could generate a fantastic volume of sound.

"How you doin', baby?" I asked Andy Maurer.

Maurer didn't answer. Fine. He had to concentrate on the game.

I had the first plays choreographed in my mind. There was no need to allow Maurer to think he could win our individual battle. But for a play or two it would be okay.

As I've said, I always got a good jump off the ball, a

talent acquired from endless sessions of watching films, from which I learned that, in his own unique fashion, *every* quarterback reveals when the ball is going to be snapped. Joe Theisman, for example, picks up his left foot. Bert Jones stopped rotating his head.

It was more difficult discovering Craig Morton's fatal flaw, partly because he possessed so much experience (and would know how to avoid such a mistake), and partly because he'd been rendered somewhat immobile owing to regular season injuries. Since it hurt to move, he didn't move much. But he did move his head ever so slightly the instant before accepting the ball, and that's when I intended to charge. My rush began *before* the ball got snapped.

On first down I wanted to get acquainted with Andy Maurer, so I charged him like a bull. The crack of helmets could be heard all the way up in the first rows of the stands—forget the noise the crowd made. We hit heads so hard mine ached for the rest of the game. Okay. I had to show Maurer right away I wasn't afraid of him. I wanted him thinking, *This guy is crazy. I have to get set for him.*

On second down I showed Maurer the same move, which meant no move at all. I came at him like an enraged wild ram, butting heads, bouncing off, coming back to bang skulls again.

Maurer loved it. He loved people to run into him. That was his job, to absorb punishment. No one could run over this squat giant, and the Denver coaches would give him a game ball if I kept trying.

On the third down he sat strong, really dug in, a granite statue placed in the Superdome Astroturf, incapable of movement, waiting for me to come at him. This time I gave him short, quick, right-left, right-left stutter steps, a 360-degree turn, and blew past him with an inside rush. *What the hell is this?* Maurer had to be thinking. *Bring back the head-banging routine.*

On the fourth down Maurer sat strong again, with just

the slightest tilt to the inside. I paid him very little attention. I watched Craig Morton, waited for that almost imperceptible head movement, and then without the slightest fake launched myself past Maurer with an *outside* rush into the Denver backfield.

Denver's opening possession managed to reach our 33-yard line, but we were establishing precedents that would last the entire game. Claudie Minor, as expected, proved incapable of controlling Too Tall Jones; Randy White wreaked mayhem in the center of the line; and Jethro simply played Jethro, tough and always in the right place.

The Broncos got no farther than the 33. We sacked Morton—his offensive line already showing signs of a confused shambles—and Denver's punter, Bucky Dilts, booted the ball down to our 1-yard line.

Tony Hill fumbled it. *God almighty!* I thought. The defense had asked only that the offense not give away points, and losing the ball on the 1-yard line could hand Denver a gift-wrapped score. But with the sound of the crowd and the boom of approaching Bronco feet in his ears, Tony Hill recovered his own fumble. I sighed, then admonished myself, *Don't worry about the offense.*

They made it tough not to worry. Moments later Dorsett fumbled on our 19-yard line. Fortunately, center John Fitzgerald recovered.

Our defense created the first turnover. Randy White and I charged Craig Morton, intending to put him in the hospital, an event that loomed so likely that he threw the ball in a panic, right into the hands of our safety, Randy Hughes.

Starting on the Denver 25, the offense made no mistakes. On the fifth play of the short drive, Tony Dorsett swept around left end for the touchdown.

Already we had more than the 5 points the bookmakers said we deserved, but I knew things wouldn't get any better for Denver. It was this simple, forget all the complicated postgame analyses: The Bronco offensive line couldn't handle our defensive line. They couldn't compete with us physically or mentally.

Soon our defense forced another Denver turnover. Linebacker Bob Breunig tipped a Morton pass to cornerback Aaron Kyle to set up our offense on the Bronco 35. This time Roger Staubach and Company produced 3 points, an Efren Herrera field goal for a 10–0 first quarter lead.

The Denver fans amazed me. Usually a crowd grows subdued when its team gets manhandled. But these people didn't lose a decibel of noise, although there were precious few plays for them to cheer.

Randy and I reached deep into our bag of tricks to keep the Broncos reeling. Especially effective were our "Limbo" and "Reverse Limbo" plays. On "Limbo," I'd fake an outside rush, simultaneous with Randy driving into the guard/tackle gap. Then I'd pivot to the inside, and the dogged Andy Maurer would go with me. The trouble for him was he'd run into Randy White, creating a huge pileup and leaving the inside rush route open for me.

On "Reverse Limbo," I'd charge straight at Maurer, then slide a little to my right. Randy would be in the middle of a looping outside rush, and I'd grab and hold his man, guard Tom Glassic. Of course, Maurer would be clinging to me for dear life—he'd be damned if I went by him again—and with my easily overlooked illegal hold on Glassic, nothing but green Astroturf separated a nervous Craig Morton from our maniacal Randy White.

Instilling fear in a quarterback ranked high on our list of priorities, and Morton knew it. We didn't maliciously attempt to injure him, but on the other hand, we didn't deliberately try not to. Morton's backup, Norris Weese, was virtually unknown (we knew him as erratic and inexperienced), so if our former teammate went down, the Broncos would face an almost hopeless situation.

My illegal holding was very unlikely to be called. When did you last see a defensive lineman get nailed for holding? I considered it merely a payback to all the offensive people who'd gotten away with much worse against me, including strangleholds and tackling. If the rules were strictly enforced, holding penalties against the offensive line could be called on almost every down.

I understood the offensive guy's point of view. If his man gets by him too often, planting stark terror in the heart of his quarterback, then his coach will find someone else to play his position. So the offensive lineman holds every time he can. He may be underpaid—are there enough bucks to repay a bone-bending battle with the terrifying Too Tall Jones for three hours of a Sunday afternoon?—but he knows he probably can't earn more at anything else. He holds. He'd do a lot more if he could get away with it. And I hold—especially during a Super Bowl with the chance to put Randy White in Craig Morton's face.

Craig never had a prayer against us. I thought he performed courageously, but what could he do? We were all over him with fearful hits, sometimes before he could drop back and get set in the pocket.

Eventually, hurt and confused, Morton was taken out and replaced by Norris Weese. Soon thereafter I sacked Weese and we recovered his fumble.

I felt no compassion for Morton. The Broncos made good on their boast to knock Tony Dorsett out of action, and Staubach broke the tip of his right forefinger, making it almost impossible for him to pass.

The Broncos committed a record (it should stand forever) *seven turnovers,* four interceptions, and three fumbles—in the *first half alone.* I don't believe any of these were uncaused turnovers. Unrelenting pressure, or the fear of it, made them as jittery as high school freshmen on a first date.

Our offense didn't cause any hearts to race, certainly not in the first half. We kept turning the ball over to the offense in excellent field position, and they missed opportunity after opportunity to score. Denver's fine linebacking corps—Bob Swenson, Joe Rizzo, Randy Gradishar, Tom Jackson—deserve much of the credit. Efren Herrera missed three field goals in the second quarter, from 43, 32, and 43 yards, and made one from 43.

At half time, we led 13–0. We played the second half just to make it official.

The game's final score, 27–10, suggests a closer contest than actually took place. Of the many lopsided statistics that stand out in my mind, the most telling was that Denver *in the entire game* made only one first down passing.

With about four minutes to go, I heard sports announcer Pat Summerall's voice come over the public address system: "And the Most Valuable Players in Super Bowl XII are . . . Randy White and Harvey Martin of the Dallas Cowboys!"

It was the absolute highwater mark of my career— what more could a football player accomplish? I thought, *It can't be true. You've heard it wrong.* That was it, I'd heard it wrong. My hearing was impaired by those Bronco fans, still yelling themselves hoarse in a cause long ago lost. Defensive players *never*—well, almost never—win MVP awards. But a lot of people on the sidelines were smiling at me, pounding my back. It had happened. For at least this one all-important game, I'd been voted Best of the Best, along with Randy.

I went right over to Randy White and put my arm around him. But I couldn't think of anything profound to say.

"I don't believe it," is all that came out of my mouth.

"I don't believe it either," said an equally eloquent Randy.

The Cowboys didn't let up much in the second half. We had fun, relaxing a little (but just a little) the way a good championship team will, knowing the opponent couldn't beat us, and savoring our moments in the Super Bowl showcase.

I still have treasured memories of that second half. I will *never* forget Pat Summerall's voice coming over the public address system. But if determining the winner was why we played the game, we could all have gone home at half time.

The city of Dallas gave us an enormous parade as World Champions when we returned home after our Super Bowl XII win over the Broncos. But it wasn't just the parade. It became impossible to go anywhere and pay for anything, even a new car. Automobile dealers gave many players a car in exchange for their endorsement of the dealership.

I received fifteen to twenty party invitations a day, although these events were tame compared to the gatherings at Too Tall's.

During the same period I served as a spokesperson for the Multiple Sclerosis Society, doing radio and TV spots and heading up fundraisers.

After the Super Bowl, I finally got around to having corrective surgery for my congenital jaw deformity. An estimated 10 million Americans suffer from a similar condition, though most not as seriously as I did. My mother first noticed my problem in my seventh grade year and mentioned it to my grandmother, who said, "You know how kids are. They always go through these changes when they're growing up."

But each year my jaw got worse. Classmates began calling me "Monkeybear." I developed an open-mouthed smile to hide the fact that my teeth didn't line up right. As I told *People* magazine, which interviewed me after my surgery, "If you add an inch and one-half to your bottom jaw, thrust it forward a lot, and then throw in a lisp, you'll have an idea of what I was like."

My top teeth were also splayed. If I took a bite out of an apple, I'd have to twist and work the chunk to get it out. I wouldn't order certain foods in public—thin things like pizza. With pizza, for instance, I couldn't take a normal bite. I'd have to stick the slice between my front teeth and then twist off a piece.

After the operation, a complete success, my mouth stayed wired shut for seven weeks. I bought a cheeseburger first thing when the wires came off but couldn't open my mouth wide enough, so I had to break the burger into pieces. When I showed up for preseason practice that spring, I weighed only 214 pounds, my clothes didn't fit, and I knew I looked terrible.

"You really look totally different," said veteran running back Robert Newhouse. "You look one hundred percent better."

Robert meant well, but he made me feel worse. I didn't like the way I looked at a skeletal 214 pounds. I must have appeared hideous before. Gradually, however, I became more outgoing and sure of myself, finally granting the interview to *People* so others, some of whom might not even know they had the problem, would see there was hope.

Much of the off-season following our Super Bowl XII triumph was spent going to various cities collecting awards. To one of these in Kansas City I took Robin, a gorgeous girl I met at the Playboy Club. When Sharon Bell found out about me and Robin, she got pissed off. Earlier, she'd learned, I'd taken another girl, Debbie, to the Pro Bowl.

Sharon didn't know about the wild parties at Too Tall's, preceded by our making the rounds of the nightclubs. I shuddered to think of her reaction if she found out about all that. Trips with Robin and Debbie were minor peccadilloes in comparison.

My near inability to pay for anything when I went out extended to every major city in America. Everything was on the house. I always insisted on paying, unless the haggle over money threatened to become absolutely embarrassing to me and the restaurant owner. On those occasions I'd always leave a tip for the waiter equivalent to the amount of the bill. I prided myself on never taking advantage of anybody, and I didn't intend to start even if someone insisted. I stopped going to certain nightclubs in Dallas simply because they never let me pay my own way.

My night life picked up. Often I went to Playmakers Plaza at Knox and McKinney, a nightclub Too Tall and Hollywood opened. The two of them, with me also taking advantage of the action, now picked up girls from their own club, their own collection.

I began smoking pot—nothing heavier than that—and so did several other Cowboys. Henderson, of course, plunged deeper into much more serious dope. Finally Too Tall, who never used anything, told him to move out.

Henderson had been going with perhaps the most beautiful woman I've ever seen, a Playboy Bunny named Wyetta, maybe the only female I'd met who had any chance at all with him—at least at first, when Hollywood wanted her more than she wanted him. His inability to impress Wyetta with his good looks, great physique, fat wallet, and Super Bowl rings made him pursue her all the more ardently. Wyetta lipped off to Thomas something good, but all this changed once Wyetta fell in love with him. She had his child, later married him . . . and lived through hell. Marriage couldn't settle him down.

Before they married—but after she had his daughter—he told her, "We can get married, but I'll always be a bachelor, no matter what. I can treat you nice, pay your rent, buy you clothes, but I ain't gonna stop fooling around."

Henderson wrote in *Playboy* magazine:

> And she was so jealous. She caught me with other women a couple times, and she'd scream and call me a bunch of names and act crazy. A couple of times I had to hold her back from jumping on the women. And she particularly disliked white women. Whenever we had an argument, she'd holler at me, "Why don't you go sleep with your white girls?" I'd say, "I think I will," and I would.

Drugs blanketed Dallas at this time. You could order them from waiters in the fanciest nightclubs, if you knew how to ask. You could pretend to be ordering from the menu and actually be buying cocaine.

Even after the opening of Playmakers Plaza, we continued to visit other clubs in our roundup of girls. When we finally got back to Too Tall's house, still more women would arrive throughout the night. Acquaintances of ours used our names as lures to bring girls over, knowing they'd score just from what we left over.

Too Tall, Thomas, and I became known at nightclubs all around town. We held forth like kings; a whole section of a nightclub might be roped apart for us to have our fun. Both white and black members of the Cowboys, their names unmentioned here to protect marriages, joined us in the partying.

On several occasions drunken bar patrons tried to pick a fight with one or another of us. Amazing. Some little loudmouth, barely able to stand, would challenge me or Too Tall to a fight, probably to impress a girl friend. But it couldn't have worked out that way. Too Tall or I could have killed him in an instant with just one hand.

Of course, we never responded to the offers to fight. We walked away. If we'd ever so much as slap a rude, obnoxious drunk, he'd have been in his lawyer's office the moment he sobered up.

Also hard to ignore were people who, to prove themselves tough, deliberately bumped into us, pretending it was an accident. They fantasized, but their fantasy would have been a nightmare if we'd responded. We never allowed ourselves to drink too much when we went out.

Too Tall, the most consistent drinker I've ever seen, never touched anything stronger than beer. He was the Cowboy beer-drinking champion. One evening on a flight home from a Sunday victory, he was challenged to a drinking contest by defensive tackle Greg Schaum. Too Tall drank a case of beer in two and one-half hours. Schaum was the one who had to be carried off the plane. When Too Tall, cold sober, arrived in the airport lobby, he asked if I planned to go out with him that night.

So many people began showing up at Too Tall's that he experienced parking problems. He finally got fed up with my skimming the crème de la crème of the girls, and let me know it wouldn't upset him if I didn't show up anymore. My straight-talking friend never had trouble making himself understood. I admired his honesty. In relating to me he was as direct as one of his fear-producing charges at an offensive back.

However, all the hijinks came *after a victory,* only after we won. If we lost a game, we asked that the lights be dimmed on the plane, and it never occurred to anyone to think about having a good time. Later, toward the end of my career, I noticed that players partied after a *loss.* This seemingly insignificant little difference between the Cowboys of 1977 and the Cowboys of, say, 1983, speaks volumes about the competitive difference between the teams. The world championship 1977 team *cared* much more. The game was always first in our minds.

I figured 1978 would be as good a year on the football field as 1977, and it almost happened. Because we held the Super Bowl championship, we were assigned the toughest schedule in the NFL, and we knew everybody was gunning for us.

I had a 1978 salary of $125,000, making me the highest paid Cowboy lineman.

At training camp that year, I spent a lot of time with offensive lineman John Fitzgerald from Boston College, a nice guy, once possessed of 4:8 speed but now slowed by knee injuries. Fitzie and I came from the old school of hard work on the football field, believing everything should be done in the context of how it helped the team.

Fitzgerald and I drank beer together after practice, and inevitably the conversation swung to how it had been in the "old days," the days of Lilly and Lee Roy.

An important realization should have dawned on me, but didn't. What I sensed subconsciously but couldn't grasp and hold, the way I might a football, were subtle changes just beginning to appear. All the talk with Fitzie about the old-time Cowboys was an unconscious comparison with the new players. I came to realize that to some of these a good time meant more than winning; to Jethro Pugh and Mel Renfro *winning* meant a good time.

Guys who didn't really deserve to be on the same field with players like Lee Roy Jordan were making a lot more money than Lee Roy ever had. I suppose many of the new Cowboys merely reflected what the press called "the Me Generation," people looking out for Number One largely to the exclusion of others around them.

Coach Landry often said, "If you don't work hard all

week, you won't play good on Sunday,'' and nothing in football could be more true. But cut-corner guys began to appear on the Cowboy roster. If one of these had even a slight injury, he wouldn't practice. Hell, if NFL players didn't practice with injuries, they'd never practice. At times Too Tall and I were the only *practicing* defensive ends.

The work habits of many of the new players were different. While an old veteran like Preston Pearson would stay up till all hours of the night studying the moves of defensive backs, new members of the Cowboys thought their day ended once the team meetings were over. We had gone by an unwritten rule that our day was over only when the season ended.

Several members of the new generation actually believed that they were something special simply because they were Dallas Cowboys, that the magic of the Cowboys attached automatically to them. They thought the star on the side of their helmet assured them of winning. Exactly the opposite was true: Every team in the NFL wanted to shoot that star off their heads.

They didn't understand that the magic of the Cowboys was earned through hard work—by someone like Too Tall bandaging up his own hand when bones jutted out and going back on the field to play, or Lee Roy risking a broken neck banging freight train Miami running back Larry Csonka head-on. And, yes, by someone like Roger, later knocked unconscious five times in a single season, coming back to win a game we had as good as lost. To continue the magic required more than merely putting on the Silver and Blue.

Coach Landry made a key move in 1978. He sent Golden Richards, the wide receiver the Steelers had beaten on so unmercifully in Super Bowl X, to the Chicago Bears. Tony "Thrill" Hill replaced Golden in the starting lineup.

Butch Johnson got inserted as Drew Pearson's backup. That was the only move Landry ever made that I disagreed with 100 percent. Butch was much tougher than Tony Hill, who did not want to run pass patterns across the middle, where he risked getting his head torn off by some pile-driving defensive back. Butch would go right over the middle. I remember Thomas Henderson going up to Tony Hill one time and saying what many of us thought: "You ought to go to the Wizard of Oz and ask him for some courage."

During the off-season, I opened a nightclub called Lucifer's, along with former WFL player Jerry Ellison and his brother Louis. We intended to cater to blacks, but whites would certainly be welcome. Black nightclubs in Dallas were generally poorly lit, often run-down, and not the kind of places you'd want to take a special date. And when blacks went to white nightclubs, they often got turned away. My own sister, Mary, had been refused entrance to a white nightclub. I went there on my own, hoping they'd deny *me* admittance, but of course I was Super Bowl co-MVP and they rolled out the red carpet.

We made Lucifer's attractive enough to compete with the finest white clubs. Every Tuesday night we held a dance contest. Radio station KNOK did live shows from the club. Whenever they performed in Dallas, Richard Pryor and Lavar Burton made Lucifer's their home away from home.

Lucifer's featured good live entertainment, tasteful, expensive furnishings, and six-foot high aquariums with sharks and exotic fish as decoration.

Although we intended the nightclub to be owned in thirds by Jerry, Louis, and myself, I proved to be the only one who could get the necessary financing and ended up as 75 percent owner. Louis Ellison especially resented that people associated the club with me. When a friend called me at the club and asked to talk to me, "the owner," Louis said, "He ain't the only **** who owns this club."

The grand opening of Lucifer's occurred at the end of 1978 training camp, and many Pittsburgh Steelers and Dallas Cowboys showed up for the occasion.

Lucifer's was always full, a fun place to go, although it provided no fun for me. The drive that caused me to work a full-time job in high school and another while in college began to show negative results. I tried to juggle too many balls. My job was to be a football player. In trying to provide for life after football, I continually ran into problems. Unfortunately, Lucifer's turned out to be a disastrous business venture that eventually cost me $250,000.

However, Recipe's and Smokey John's were doing well, and there we began thinking of expansion.

The Cowboys opened the 1978 season with four wins and two losses. In the seventh game, against the Cardinals in St. Louis, my foot got caught in a pile of players and then one of the Cardinals blocked down on me. White lightning shot through my leg. For the first time in my career I screamed out in pain. I'd suffered a twisted knee, but it could have been much worse, torn ligaments or cartilage.

I continued to play in the game and bruised my thigh sacking Jim Hart. He ducked just as I intended to clobber him and his helmet hit my thigh, causing a bad bone bruise. Throughout my career, I was always hurting Hart, or vice versa.

I stayed in the game, spurred on by the St. Louis fans, who genuinely hated me because I sacked their quarterback so often. I would have felt terrible if they hadn't hated me. Later in the game I knocked Jim Hart out of action for the rest of the afternoon with a clean hit, and we won 24–21.

The next week I tried to play against the Eagles in Dallas with my right knee heavily taped. When on the first play I attempted to stand up offensive tackle Stan Walters, the knee gave out. I couldn't put any weight on it, much less play football. That week the Cowboys flew me to New York City to get a "Joe Namath" knee brace. I made three trips to the Big Apple that year.

On my first trip to New York—Randy White and I went there to pick up the new Thunderbird automobiles we'd been awarded as co-MVPs of the Super Bowl—I went to Studio 54. I got dressed up in my best Dallas going-out clothes, which were hardly the fashion in Manhattan. Studio 54 was jammed. A big doorman outside selected people to come in. It wasn't a question of waiting in line; he'd just pick people at random and wave them inside.

"I want to go in," I told him when I caught his eye.

"You can't," he said.

I never used my name to gain entrance anywhere (in Dallas I didn't have to), but I really wanted to see Studio 54. Employing the ruse of a modern Ali Baba, I voiced the magic words I was sure would open the hermetically sealed chamber: "O.J. told me I should come here."

"I'm sorry," the doorman said.

So I went to New York, New York, instead and had a good time.

At an awards ceremony the next day a reporter asked, "How'd you like Studio 54?"

"They wouldn't let me in," I said.

The story appeared in *Time, Newsweek, The New York Times*—all over the country: Harvey Martin, Super Bowl co-MVP, refused admittance to Studio 54. I emphasized it hadn't been a race thing. The guy at the door just considered me too conservatively dressed.

The management of Studio 54 sent me a letter of apology, and urged me to visit the next time I was in town.

On my second trip to New York City, Jeanette Kahn, president of Warner Comic Books, picked me up at the airport. She'd written me earlier, on Superman stationery, proposing a series of Harvey Martin "Martinizing" comic books, in which I'd be depicted as a derring-do jock, catching criminals and defending the downtrodden.

While in the city I attended a banquet given by *Sports Illustrated*. On the bus the magazine provided to transport athletes from the hotel to the charity dinner, I sat next to NBA scoring machine Bob McAdoo.

"What you gonna do tonight?" McAdoo asked.

"I'm going to Studio 54 with Jeanette Kahn," I said.

"Oh yeah?"

"Why don't you go with us?"

"You really want me to?" he said. I thought it strange that he seemed so insecure about the whole affair. "You sure I can come along?" he kept asking.

I rode to McAdoo's hotel in his magnificent Excaliber, and called Jeanette from his room. "Bob McAdoo would like to go with us tonight."

I could feel the tension on the other end of the line. "Is Bob with you now?" Jeanette asked, lowering her voice.

"Yes."

"Harvey, I date Bob McAdoo."

"It'll be okay," I said, keeping a straight face. I hung up and looked across at the anxious McAdoo, then burst out laughing.

"You wanted to see if I had anything going with Jeanette, didn't you?" I said between gales of laughter.

"I guess so," he said sheepishly.

"And that's why you wanted to come along, right?"

"I suppose."

The three of us went to the world-famous disco that night and had a lot of fun.

On my third trip to New York—to get the knee brace—I again visited my friend Jeanette at her home. We had a good time, ordering in cartons of delicious Chinese food, and talking about our lives. I couldn't help but think of Sharon Bell. Like her, Jeanette was cultured and highly intelligent. I figured I still played the fool not asking Sharon to marry me, but selfishly couldn't bring myself to give up the great times I was having. And I knew neither Sharon nor I could live in a have-my-cake-and-eat-it-too marriage.

The next Sunday I saw a lot of action, but didn't play well, in a game we lost to Minnesota 21–10. My knee swelled up terribly, but I didn't tell anyone. Landry ultimately replaced me with Larry Bethea.

I turned my season around the following week, when Miami defeated us 23–16 in the Orange Bowl. My thigh, swollen to twice its normal size, was wrapped in more tape than a mummy's, and my swollen knee had the Joe Namath brace strapped around it. I'd been throwing up at home, and did so again before the Miami game.

To hell with it, I thought. I threw the brace away. It only hindered my movement and slowed me down. I played the whole game without it. Bethea came in on short yardage situations, which my knee simply couldn't withstand. But I could play at all other times, though occasionally I thought the pain might cause me to black out.

After the Miami loss, we won our last six regular season games, bulldozing five of the opponents:

Cowboys	42
Green Bay	14
Cowboys	27
New Orleans	7
Cowboys	37
Washington	10
Cowboys	17
New England	10
Cowboys	31
Philadelphia	13
Cowboys	30
Jets	7

That season Thomas Henderson turned into what I call a creature. He screamed at everybody, teammates and opponents alike. Some of us called him the Prophet, because he told our opponents in advance, à la Muhammad Ali, what we were going to do to them; and then we went out and did it.

We defeated Atlanta 27–20 in the divisional playoff game and crushed the Rams 28–0 to win the NFC championship, thereby qualifying for a second straight Super Bowl, our third in four years.

I enjoyed Henderson's cocky bragging, but others didn't. Just before the end of the slaughter of the Rams for the NFC championship, Too Tall went over to Henderson and said, "Thomas, you're going to have to shut up, man. You're gonna wear us all out. We had to come out here and work ourselves to death just backing up all the things you said. I'm tired and wish you would just cool it. Keep talking like that and we'll have to play so hard against Pittsburgh in the Super Bowl that it'll take us a week to recover."

Henderson had intercepted a pass against the Rams and run it back for a touchdown, icing the cake with a slam dunk over the crossbar. *Great!* I thought. *Stick it in their eye!*

Too Tall wasn't impressed. He'd lived with Hollywood and knew the man much better than I did.

The Steelers ate up the AFC in the 1978 season and viewed our championship in Super Bowl XII as an insignificant, unscheduled stop of their express train ride to Team of the Decade honors. That's precisely how the game shaped up: as more than a Super Bowl, as a battle for recognition as best team of the 1970s. Close observers of football predicted the finest Super Bowl ever played, and they were right.

We were the defending World Champions, but the Steelers showed us no respect. That's one of the reasons I smiled when Henderson baited them back, saying Terry Bradshaw's brain was so dense he couldn't spell *cat* if you spotted him the C and the T. Dallas sportswriters worried that Henderson's mouth would fire up the Steelers, but I didn't care; I knew they'd be fired up anyway. I'd gotten tired of hearing them praised. We'd had a tougher schedule and cruised to the Super Bowl just as easily as they had.

I telephoned Dwight White a week or so before the game. "We're gonna kick your ass," I told him when he answered.

"You'll never kick our asses with Roger at quarterback," Dwight said, echoing the deeply held but erroneous belief of many of the Steelers that Staubach didn't deserve respect. They felt this way, I think, because Roger wouldn't sit in a cafe, like Ernie Holmes, and down two fifths of cognac in a single night.

In addition, Dwight felt he owned our offensive tackle Pat Donovan, who had replaced Ralph Neely, and that

Rayfield had grown old and would be demolished by L. C. Greenwood. Dwight also predicted Roger would "remember the beating we gave him in Super Bowl X," and be gun shy.

I didn't think any of this made sense, but that's why they run betting pools.

Thomas Henderson continued to pop off the entire week before the Super Bowl, talking himself right onto the cover of *Newsweek* magazine. One newspaper called the game "the Henderson Super Bowl." It was hardly that.

Skip Bayless, a Dallas newspaper columnist, viewed it another way: "It's macho versus chivalry. Blood and guts versus head and heart. Ugly versus pretty. Snarls versus smiles."

That the Steelers were rough, even vicious, I didn't doubt, but we weren't the altar boys Bayless described. I for one intended to use every tactic I knew, fair or foul, to win this game. It wasn't the Henderson Super Bowl or a struggle between good and evil. It really was a battle for recognition as Team of the Decade, a form of immortality, I imagined.

We tried to play mind games with the officials the week before Super Bowl XIII. Even at this late date, none of us could believe the Steelers hadn't received a single penalty in the Super Bowl X game against us, and we hoped to avoid a repeat of that sorry performance by the referees.

Drew Pearson made a point of reminding the press of a dozen penalties that should have been called in Super Bowl X but weren't. Charlie Waters said the Super Bowl X officials had "choked." Even Coach Landry, who never complains, said the Steelers "got away with a good thing in 1976. Let's just hope it doesn't happen again."

I didn't think the officials choked or tried to "get" us in

Super Bowl X. I felt they simply were in over their heads.

Unbelievably, unlike major league baseball and the NBA, the NFL does not have officials whose only job it is to referee games. The powers-that-be in basketball and baseball have officials who officiate and do nothing else, who devote full-time to understanding the game and its rules. To save a few dollars, I assume, the NFL hires "officials" who in everyday life are lawyers, doctors, and insurance salesmen. Players spend most of their productive lives developing skills to their ultimate, but any game, even a Super Bowl, can be lost when a part-time referee straight out of a hospital operating room or a courtroom makes an incorrect decision.

I believe when Bobby Fischer played for and won world championships at chess, the judges of those matches were chess grandmasters who'd devoted their lives to understanding the intricacies of the game.

Every football player dreams of reaching the Super Bowl, the ultimate game, and his ultimate dream is to win it. Referees should not be allowed to stand in the way of the dream's fulfillment.

Still, although the NFL in 1986 is introducing television replays whereby the decisions of officials can be questioned, I have mixed emotions about this innovation, too. I think it will slow up the game, and take away the factor of human error, which has a place in sports. Surely the players are not perfect. Even Jethro Pugh, who always strove for perfection, admittedly came up short. Wouldn't a better solution be for the NFL to open its bulging coffers and spend the money necessary to make its officials as professional as its players?

If I were fixing a football game, I would want a referee in my corner. Referees are in the best position of anyone to alter the outcome of a game, and for that very reason the NFL should move heaven and earth to assure that, like Caesar's wife, they are above suspicion.

Even a quarterback does not have the life-and-death control over a game that the official has. If a quarterback continues to make mistakes, the coach likely will replace him. But nobody replaces an official. He's in action the entire game. The way pro football is played, the official can nullify *any* play with a holding call. A few strategically placed holding calls can break the back of any team.

For example, in Super Bowl XX, the officials mistakenly made calls—or non-calls—that gave the Bears 10 additional points. Three of these points resulted from the officials' not even knowing the rules, or at least not thinking to enforce the rules at the time. On another day those 10 points could have been the difference between winning and losing.

The refs should work as long and hard as we do. Let them play on knees smashed to mush, and see how they like losing the world championship because of a bad call.

Super Bowl XIII is still remembered as the most exciting ever played. Here were two great teams at the peak of their physical and mental capabilities, teams that, against any other, would have waltzed to the championship as easily as we did against Denver.

I was matched against Jon Kolb, perhaps the strongest offensive tackle in football and probably the best I ever went up against. Oddly enough, Kolb didn't give me the most trouble. Kolb was a muscle man, a *specimen,* and I always enjoyed playing against that type.

The offensive tackle I had the most trouble with in my career was Stan Walters of the Philadelphia Eagles, a very unorthodox, "soft" lineman. Walters, larger than most offensive tackles, never charged a defensive end. Instead he floated like a boxer, dancing this way and that, always between me and the quarterback. I went nuts playing pitty-pat with Walters.

One thing wouldn't change: Coach Landry again counseled us not to fight back when the Steelers used their extra-rough tactics. Landry hoped all our pregame talk urging the officials to keep an eye out for the dirty stuff would have an effect.

We trailed the Steelers 21–17 entering the fourth quarter in this brutal "superest of Super Bowls," but momentum had swung in our favor. I think even Pittsburgh knew it. The game would have been tied except that our veteran tight end Jackie Smith, standing all alone in the end zone, dropped an easy pass from Roger. No matter! The Steelers knew we were making them eat that "sissy" talk.

Our defense continually put heat on Bradshaw, and I knew it was only a matter of moments until the Steelers would turn the ball over to us!

Bradshaw dropped back to pass and we came after him, holding nothing in reserve, intending to knock him out of the game for good, just as we did in Super Bowl X. In desperation he threw the ball away, throwing it as long and as far as he could. What I saw next—I do not exaggerate—almost made me die.

I saw Lynn Swann run under the pass Bradshaw had merely tried to throw away to avoid an injury or a sack, or both . . . Lynn Swann run up the back of our defender Benny Barnes, an obvious offensive interference . . . and referee Fred Swearingen throw a flag from what seemed a mile away and call Barnes for *defensive* interference. The call gave the Steelers a first down on our 23-yard line.

It was a hideous, killing call for us.

But don't take just my word for it. Listen to what Roger Staubach, the most careful and truthful of men, had to say in his book, *Time Enough to Win:*

I never could figure out how Benny could be running fullblast downfield and intentionally trip a receiver *behind* him, which is where Swann was. The whole thing took place near our bench. I was standing right there and saw it. When I saw the flag I thought it was interference on Swann for pushing or something like that.

The official right on the play was back judge Pat Knight. He made the first signal, waving his arms back and forth for an incompletion. Then here came the flag from over in the middle of the field. All our guys started yelling because they thought it was interference on Swann. Incredibly, field judge Fred Swearingen saw the play differently from everybody else in the Orange Bowl. . . .

That whole chain of events was ironic. Swann's play was the biggest of the drive yet wasn't the result of anything he did. It was some idiot official throwing a flag when he'd been out of position to see the play right. And another official standing on top of the play allowing himself to be talked into a penalty that wasn't there.

Fred Swearingen's call was so horrible that NFL Commissioner Pete Roselle made an unprecedented public admission that the penalty had been wrong. But of course this came days after the game—after the players and fans had gone home, after the outcome had been decided, after our hearts were already broken.

Shortly after Swearingen gave the ball to the Steelers deep in our territory, Franco Harris raced over my position for a touchdown. I don't think it's second-guessing to say I would have stopped that play if I'd been in the game. But I wasn't; it was physically impossible. Just before Franco's run I'd had to come out with a pulled hamstring.

The awesome Steelers were the very lucky Steelers that day. We fumbled the kickoff after Franco's touchdown—somehow it skittered erratically to Randy White, who was playing with a broken thumb—and the Steelers turned the fumble into a touchdown and a 35–17 lead.

A rout? Hardly.

Less than seven minutes remained, but if the Cowboys stood for anything, it was "Never say die." And Roger and the offense almost pulled it off.

At the end of the game the Steelers, who'd called *us* sissies, didn't know one end of the field from the other. They resembled punch-drunk fighters trying desperately to hold on, hoping the final bell would ring.

First Roger threw a touchdown pass to Billy Joe DuPree, then another to Butch Johnson. And he would have thrown another and another . . . except that time ran out with Terry Bradshaw taking a snap from center, curling his body into the fetal position, and going down intentionally to run out the last few seconds.

The 35–31 Pittsburgh victory should have been a 31–21 Cowboy win. Fred Swearingen gave the Steelers their fourth touchdown, and they scored their fifth because of the Randy White fumble, which never could have happened if they hadn't scored the fourth. We wouldn't have been receiving, so Randy White wouldn't have fumbled, and so on and so forth . . .

Sportswriters voted the Steelers the Team of the Decade, even though the Cowboys had a better win/loss record during the 1970s.

Pittsburgh won four Super Bowls while the Cowboys took two. Many Cowboys, myself included, will argue that by rights those numbers should be reversed. Or how about this: Cowboys 2, Steelers 2, Zebras (officials) 2?

I walked off the field when the final gun sounded, wanting to play some more, cursing the clock. Suddenly old pal Dwight White was there administering one of his hugs. "You played hard," he said, exactly what he'd told me after Super Bowl X.

Instead of dying I went to my hotel room alone, lay on my bed, and let dizzying waves of depression sweep over me. I kept having to get up and weave my way to the bathroom to vomit. The game results literally made me sick. After a while I could hear the half-hearted noises of our losers' party downstairs. I knew Mom expected to see me, so I headed down. When Mom saw me, she came over and put her arms around me and, in her loving, maternal way, gave me the comfort I needed for the hurt I felt.

increased my business activities dramatically during the off-season after Super Bowl XIII. WFAA Radio hired me with an oral promise that I'd be on camera for WFAA-TV, Channel 8, the Dallas ABC affiliate. I worked on the development of St. Paul's Square, a black neighborhood renovation project in San Antonio. We also expanded Smokey John's, adding two Smokey's Expresses, smaller, quicker versions of Smokey John's. And I became a part owner of the Slender Now Corporation, which recommended and sold vitamins to supplement an individual's overall conditioning program.

In other words, I attacked the world, happy to fill every minute of my day. But I did too much, spread myself too thin. And I had no one with a good business head to warn me of this simple fact. If anything, the opposite held true. At a time when I should have been cutting back, more and more people came to me with ideas for new investments, new activities.

I became the black radio voice for 7-Eleven nationwide, a job that gave me considerable satisfaction, but I never got identified by name as the person doing the commercials. My skills as an announcer were sufficient that I didn't have to rely on my name. For all the listener knew, I could have been an unknown struggling black actor. I never told anyone the voice they heard on radio was mine, and only one Cowboy, Butch Johnson, ever figured it out.

I did soft drink ads and commercials on TV. My "Y'all thirsty?" for Orange Crush became a trademark in Dallas. At Texas Stadium I once turned to look up into the stands and a whole section of the crowd shouted at me, "Y'all thirsty?"

I actually worked and played myself out of a job with Dr. Pepper. Orange Crush, whose formula Dr. Pepper bought, became so popular in minority areas it really didn't have to advertise to sell. Moreover, Dr. Pepper executives figured there couldn't be a less likely person in the world than me to continue selling Orange Crush. Denver's defense had become known across the nation as the Orange Crush, and as co-MVP in Super Bowl XII, my name was associated with crushing the orange of Denver. Moreover, I'd been off to the side smiling when Hollywood Henderson, toward the end of the game, was seen by America's largest viewing audience crushing an Orange Crush cup in his hand to symbolize what we'd done to the Broncos.

I went to WFAA because it paid twice as much as KRLD—but especially because I'd been promised TV time. Once there, I got the runaround whenever I asked about the television part of the deal. My radio show was syndicated all over Texas, and I conducted some hilarious interviews with Too Tall.

As for our football chances in 1979, we received the worst possible news. Too Tall Jones, whose contract had expired, announced that he had decided to become a professional boxer. Sportswriters speculated that this was just a ploy to win a fat contract, but I never believed that for a moment. Too Tall was always straightforward; he never bluffed. If he said he wanted to be a boxer, that's what he wanted. I saw Too Tall make his announcement during a press conference with heavyweight champ Larry

Holmes. I must say, Holmes didn't look particularly terrified.

I didn't know how to gauge Too Tall's chances as a fighter. He'd never boxed before. I did know a tougher person couldn't exist and that he possessed a long reach—and the biggest heart on the planet when he was off the field.

On the field it was another story. "I'm going to get that old SOB," he said of Cardinals tackle Ernie McMillan in a game against St. Louis. He then promptly ran over McMillan the way a car runs over a weed, knocking McMillan out of the game, and out of football. Too Tall's charge ended McMillan's career; I don't believe he ever played another down.

"Looks like you'll have to handle it," I said to Larry Bethea at the Cowboy training center.

"I can do it! I can do it!" Bethea bubbled.

I looked at him and wondered. He floated in seventh heaven. Bethea had good football skills, but I couldn't help thinking, *there's only one Too Tall.*

I thought a lot about Too Tall during that off-season. Too Tall and Harvey, Harvey and Too Tall—the names seemed to me to belong together. It was hard to imagine football without him, but I knew a man had to do what's best for himself.

Hadn't Landry himself said it a thousand times? "In this business . . ." Landry began many of his sentences, and that was just it. It was a *business,* despite all the fun and games. To the credit of Cowboy management, which, like any other professional franchise, would love the player to look at pro football as just a game, while they knew differently, I didn't hear any complaints about Too Tall abandoning the team at the peak of his career. All Landry said at the start of training camp was, "We've had a big loss."

Obviously major adjustments would have to be made on the defensive line. Larry Cole took up some of the slack, doing a bang-up job, but David Stalls was a disappointment to me. I didn't think he wanted to pay the price I knew necessary. A nice guy, Stalls. But I feared he wouldn't do his share.

Rookie Ron Springs caught my eye right away. Each year there's always some hell-bent-for-leather rookie who attracts attention right away (a recent example is special teams star Bill Bates), and this year Springs filled the bill. My first impression of Springs was that Hollywood Henderson didn't like him, which meant he couldn't be all bad. My second impression: Springs didn't like Thomas Henderson. Henderson, screaming and crazy, singled out Springs for repeated administration of punishment, but Springs never took a backward step. The harder Henderson hit Springs, the harder this tough cocky rookie gave back at Hollywood.

The defensive front four Landry intended to play consisted of Larry Bethea and me at ends and Larry Cole and Randy White at tackles. Later we acquired John Dutton (an All-Pro from the Baltimore Colts), but Dutton was frequently injured during the 1979 season.

With Too Tall gone, I spent more time than ever with Drew Pearson, the worst judge of defensive backfield talent who ever lived. I often asked Drew his opinion of various defensive backs on our team and others, and his answer always came back the same: Nobody was any good. Drew didn't think a good defensive back had been born yet, and I soon realized he was the wrong person to ask. Drew had such great talent that he could beat anyone in single coverage, which provided scarcely any challenge for him; consequently he didn't think *anybody* had much ability.

In our suite in the Thousand Oaks dorm—on the second floor, with a breathtaking view of the mountains that was especially beautiful at sunset—I roomed with Benny Barnes, Billy Joe DuPree, and Drew. Drew and I were free spirits, often sneaking out after hours to see girls. As rookies we couldn't get away with anything, but as veterans who'd learned the ropes we were too smart for any coach to catch.

In the old dorm all we needed to do was lam it out a window and through some bushes to freedom. But in the new dorm we had to go through a parking lot that overlooked the coaches' rooms. Getting out in 1979 required some thinking.

Preston Pearson, who seldom sneaked out in his fourteen-year career, nonetheless knew many of the moves:

Okay, if you see a player walking around a hotel lobby during the day, collecting books of matches, you are not to assume he is either a heavy smoker or a matchbook cover collector. What he's doing is collecting them to use as wedges in the side door exits. Of course, the doors are all supposed to self-lock at night, so you have to spend a great deal of time during the day planning your get-away. I remember a guy who wedged matchbooks into doors for eighteen floors so that he could get away via the fire exit stairs. Then, you have to stash a change of clothes somewhere on the first floor. See, what you have to do is sneak out in your underwear so if you're caught on the way down you can just explain to a coach that you're looking for ol' so-and-so's room. He's not going to think you're trying to sneak out when you're running around in nothing but your shorts.

We had one telephone in our suite, and fights continually erupted over who would use it. The businesslike Billy Joe DuPree needed the phone to keep track of his numerous business transactions, and he complained that Drew and I cost him "a fortune" because we tied up the phone so often talking with girls. Defensive back Benny Barnes, one of the nicest guys on the team, tried to stay clear of the fighting. Nor did Benny, a regular, ever complain about having to cover kickoffs, considered a lowly and dangerous chore, fit only for substitutes.

Thomas Henderson still sneaked girls into the dorm in 1979, but team members were generally less blatant about it than in preceding years. In 1974 Craig Morton was caught bringing two women into the dormitory by Assistant Coach Jerry Tubbs. Tubbs told the star quarterback to get them out. "Ah, Tubbs," said Morton, "I'm not going to do that." Coach Landry had to intervene to salvage this situation.

Landry employed an intricate system of fines. He had a major—and I mean major—fine for girls in the dorm. That's why the players would rather risk sneaking out, which I did frequently.

I didn't leave my car in the parking lot. That way I could still exit the back way through the bushes and link up with my transportation on a nearby street.

These nocturnal trips were strictly for female company. Both Drew and I knew drinking would only hurt us, what with a brutal Landry practice always scheduled the next morning. We rationalized that we were just part of a long and honorable Cowboy tradition. Why, even Lee Roy Jordan sneaked out once in a while. Our keys to success were waiting until coaches checked our room, and always leaving a phone number where we could be reached. If we got discovered missing, we wanted to get back fast and stop Landry's clock from running. He determined the amount of the fine by the lateness of the player.

Nor were players the only ones who violated curfew. Several times while relaxing with a girl in a quiet club, I ran into Cowboy assistant coaches. Without a word being necessary, we made a pact: All of us would keep our mouths shut. As Archie Bunker used to say so beautifully, "You wash your hands, I'll wash mine."

I always volunteered advice to rookies, which I would have done anyway, but I considered it part of my job as captain. I didn't care how big and tough a rookie looked. I knew how he felt, and I remembered how Lilly had helped me.

Many veterans won't volunteer advice to rookies, and

I understand their reasons. Many of the new generation of athletes, with their high salaries and bonuses (it's absurd when some college player *starts out* making more money than a ten-year pro veteran), thought they already knew everything.

Also, why should a veteran help a rookie who might end up taking the veteran's job? Most veterans will help rookies if they ask, but they won't often go out of their way. My attitude was that it helped the *team* if I shared what I knew with young players. But, of course, unlike a marginal veteran, who might feel differently, I didn't fear anyone taking my job. I didn't think the player capable of doing that existed.

Hollywood Henderson may have been one of the few who wouldn't give advice to young guys even if they asked. Thomas was feeling on top of the world. He had just made more than $100,000 from doing a *single* 7-Up television commercial with Pat Haden, and he bought what he considered the biggest and best house in Texas. He told me he wanted a nicer home than I had, and he filled his house with ultra-expensive furniture. "I just bought class," he'd say every time he purchased a new knickknack.

"You can't buy class," I'd tell him, but Thomas didn't listen.

"If people knew all the women I've gone to bed with," Henderson boasted, "it would shock Dallas."

I didn't doubt it. This black superstud bedded some of the richest and most socially prominent women in the city.

Thomas made super amounts of money, and spent it as fast as it came in. Money, among other things, made him lose his mind. I've never seen anyone get a bigger head.

At the opening of training camp before the 1979 season, he rented a stretch limousine and had the driver park it alongside the practice field. He sat in the back in air-conditioned comfort, sniffing coke and watching the team sweat. After about a half hour, his mind frazzled by the drug, he walked across the field, right past an unsmiling Coach Landry, greeted several of the players, returned to his limo, and left. Henderson later said this was a gambit to win himself a pay hike.

But let Henderson tell it in his own words:

All during camp, me and Landry kept having meetings, but when the season started, I still hadn't negotiated my raise. Just the same, I started out playing great. We were automatic contenders for the Super Bowl, but I didn't much want to go to practice. Part of the reason was that my coke consumption was way up, which didn't help matters on the home front, either. Wyetta and I couldn't live together, so I moved out a month after my baby was born. I'm not proud of it, but we had had a fight about my bringing two women into our apartment, and that was that. But, see, Wyetta had changed, too. I mean, I understand pregnancy, but . . . she gained a lot of weight.

I tried to talk sense to Thomas but he lived somewhere around the bend. He simply fell asleep in team meetings. He wore dark glasses, a trick all of us had learned from Jethro Pugh, along with the position to assume that allowed one to sleep while looking alert. Coach Landry immersed himself so deeply in football, what he taught us, that I don't think he knew players slept. In many ways I admire Landry for this. We were supposed to be men, and it was our responsibility to soak up what he told us. He wasn't some elementary school instructor who was expected constantly to be looking over the shoulders of recalcitrant children.

Henderson began deciding when he would practice. He showed up when he wanted to, which wasn't often. When I confronted him with how he hurt the team by not practicing, he lied to me, moaning about a multitude of aches and pains from which he suffered. While we sweated, Thomas whiled away his hours in the training room.

When Thomas didn't miss practices, he complained and became a major disruptive influence on the team. I told him frankly what I saw: a young man at the peak of his powers throwing his life away. I tried to appeal to him in a way I hoped would work. "Be real cool right now, Thomas," I said. "Stop the bitching. You may think the coaches will take it forever, but they won't. You're the best, Thomas, you're Hollywood. You can be All-Pro forever, but you can also lose it all. For your own sake, straighten yourself out."

"Okay, Harvey," he said.

But he didn't mean it. And the next day he'd spend his practice time in the training room.

Wyetta called me often, her voice more desperate each time. Thomas drove her crazy, she said. Other women were always calling and asking for him. She said Thomas was gone all the time, and she didn't know what to do. My heart went out to Wyetta, but I didn't know what to do either.

Thomas did show up for team meetings, but his nose always ran, and he'd blow huge gobs of snot and phlegm onto his T-shirt. I thought it disgusting. I didn't think he could last much longer, but just when I figured things had got to rock bottom, he'd surprise me.

Once, while Thomas was asleep during a team meeting, Landry asked him a tough question. I nudged him awake and repeated the question in a whispered voice. He came alert immediately, gave an absolutely brilliant answer, then went back to sleep.

In one early season game, a contest in which we were getting our butts kicked, Landry benched Henderson just before half time. A few moments later, unbelievably, I saw Thomas hamming it up for the TV camera, waving a bandana a friend had asked him to plug, a big grin on his face, flashing the Number One sign. I felt like throttling him right on the spot. Instead I went up to him at half time and said, "We can still win this game."

"I don't care," he said.

I looked into his eyes and could tell he didn't.

"What's the matter with you, Thomas?" I asked. But he didn't answer, and all I could do was walk away.

Landry kept Thomas out of action most of the second half, and after the game Assistant Coach Jerry Tubbs went to Henderson in the locker room to explain why he'd been kept on the bench. Tubbs was a nice guy, an original Cowboy (he'd come to the franchise in its first year), someone we all respected, but Henderson immediately started treating him like a dog. In front of the team, the coaches, everybody, Thomas shouted, "I'm Hollywood! Trade me! Every team in the world wants me! Fuck you, Tubbs! Trade me, you ****!"

I sat there, mouth agape, knowing I was watching a madman. "He's not home no more," I said to Drew. "The body's here, but the mind isn't."

On the plane home none of the players talked to Henderson or even went near him. We treated him like a leper, but he seemed unaware. He made playful passes at the flight attendants. He was still Hollywood, a big grin on his face and stewardesses on his lap. I could only wonder what terrible thing possessed him.

The sadness of the whole Hollywood Henderson drama got summed up for me as we left the airport parking lot. By coincidence I followed his car as it pulled onto the freeway. He came alongside a little Volkswagen with two girls inside. Henderson waved at them, pointed at them, shouted that he wanted them to pull over. Here was a guy with more women than Casanova, and still he had to flag down two girls on the freeway. They sensibly ignored him and kept going.

A little earlier in the season, Landry told Thomas that he wouldn't be starting the next Sunday because of missing practices. Henderson told Landry, "If I don't start, I don't play." Then Thomas came to me and related what he'd done.

"You're crazy," I said.

Amazingly, Landry backed off and let him start.

I know Coach Landry would do almost anything, even swallow his considerable pride, if he felt the slightest chance existed of helping the vastly gifted Henderson. Landry not only went the extra mile with Thomas, he went many more miles.

But Henderson burned his last bridge when he cursed out Jerry Tubbs, a decent man. The next day Thomas was gone.

At the next team meeting Coach Landry, as always, gave us a minimum of information: "We had to release Thomas," is all he said.

The day Henderson was released, he called a press conference. Landry couldn't fire him, he said, because he'd quit. I later learned he went straight from the meeting with Landry to buy a quarter bag of cocaine.

The San Francisco Forty-niners picked up Hollywood, and soon renamed him Holiday because of his habit of missing practices. One day during a workout he leaned on a goal post, seemingly oblivious to the world, and a Forty-niners coach told him to move. Henderson moved a few feet, went into what is known as a hurdler's stretch, and remained there for ten minutes. When the coach checked on him, he found Thomas had fallen asleep in the hurdler's stretch.

The Houston Oilers picked up Henderson next, and he spent much of his time with them free-basing cocaine before being released again.

Coach Don Shula of the Miami Dolphins gave Thomas his last chance in pro football, but Henderson broke his neck in a preseason game. Everything really went on the skids then. I found it very sad, when after breaking his neck, Thomas talked about making a football comeback. He ultimately got charged with a sex crime in California. I felt extremely sorry that a man with such undeniable talent had gotten himself into such difficulties and damaged a great career.

On his way to the Miami Dolphins, Thomas stopped at my home and borrowed $500, which he said he needed for tires for his car. I later learned he used the money to buy cocaine. He also borrowed money from Drew Pearson, Mike Hegman, Roger Staubach, and others. Of course, he never paid anyone back.

After his football career ended, Henderson spent time in Dallas boasting about his upcoming book. He threatened to implicate people in drug usage and sexual hijinks if they didn't pay him blackmail money. A few individuals did pay him off. No book existed, of course, and most of the people he threatened told him to go to hell.

To me, Thomas Henderson will always be a sad enigma, a great, great player who got too much too soon too fast. I've often wondered whether Too Tall could have helped if he had been around in 1979, the decisive season of Thomas's life. But Too Tall was gone, and I doubt if anyone could have saved Thomas. Besides, Too Tall had already cut off all relations with Thomas, after the linebacker, undoubtedly in a cocaine-influenced paranoia, had made the absurd accusation that Too Tall was having an affair with Wyetta.

Today Thomas lives in a California penitentiary. As the *Los Angeles Times* said, "He was once No. 56 on the cover of *Newsweek*. Now, he's C-87983," his prison number.

In Long Beach, California, in November 1983, the police came to get him, charging that he'd held a .38 caliber pistol to the head of a fifteen-year-old girl and forced her to perform oral copulation while a seventeen-year-old quadriplegic had to watch from her wheelchair. Then Thomas made matters worse by offering the girls a $10,000 bribe not to testify. He got sentenced to four years in prison. "No matter what he gets," said the quadriplegic, "it isn't enough."

I read that from prison Thomas says he wants to speak to youngsters about the evils of drugs. Before the California charges, he once said he'd found God and wanted to tell others of the marvelous experience.

A lot went wrong for the Cowboys in 1979. The problems Henderson caused and the absence of Too Tall got exacerbated by the frequency with which Roger Staubach got knocked unconscious. All of us worried a lot about Roger. We hated to see him get hurt. You'd have to understand Coach Landry to know what he meant when, after one of Roger's concussions, he said, "I was delighted it was his head and not his knee."

More seriously in 1979, fullback Robert Newhouse suffered a broken leg. *Three weeks* went by before it was correctly diagnosed. I myself would come to experience the less-than-perfect medical treatment provided by the Cowboys.

I made the Pro Bowl again that year and led the team in sacks. The Cowboys lost a heartbreaker in the divisional playoff game against the Rams, 21–19.

Our last game of the season, against the Redskins in Dallas, ranks as one of the most important we ever played. The winner made the playoffs and won the NFC East. I hated the Redskins anyway, even if the stakes hadn't been so high.

My feeling toward them and their fans wasn't improved when, during the week before the game, I received an elaborate funeral wreath from a Redskin supporter. I took the wreath with me to Texas Stadium on the day of the game, which turned out to be a brutal affair.

With just four minutes remaining, Washington led 34–21 and had the ball. Cliff Harris forced a fumble and Randy White recovered. Roger promptly hit Ron Springs with a 26-yard touchdown strike.

We got the ball back again with 1:46 remaining, 75 yards from the goal line. Down the field Roger marched us, hitting the winning touchdown with forty-five seconds remaining. It was Roger's last regular season game, and one of his greatest.

The game transformed me into a maniac. Afterward, I carried the funeral wreath to the visiting team's locker room, threw open the door, and hurled it at a cluster of players. "Take this shit back home with you!" I shouted. "You're the ones who need it now!"

The next day came meeting Number Three with Coach Landry. "What you did was gauche," he said. "You should apologize."

"They wouldn't apologize to us," I said.

Landry never changed expression. He nodded his head slowly and somberly.

But I always did what Landry said. I sent telegrams of apology to the Washington team and all the newspapers in D.C., even though I didn't feel the least bit sorry. I received thousands of hate letters from the Washington fans, despite my telegrams, which was fine with me. I didn't care for them either.

The Cowboys of the year before would easily have defeated the Rams, but 1979 was a year filled with problems. Although we didn't know it, the pass Roger completed to our offensive guard Herb Scott was the last he ever threw. It disappointed me terribly that we hadn't made the Super Bowl for a third straight year, but after a hard look at our roster I believed we'd be back the next season where I felt the Cowboys always belonged, playing for the world championship.

Major, 24-carat business problems hit me in the off-season of 1980, right after I returned from helping Ahmad Rashad with his football camp in Minnesota. I'd had a good time with Ahmad. When I arrived for the football camp, he picked me up in a 1950s Rolls Royce (he also owned a new Corniche, which he'd bought from Reggie Jackson).

I received a call from my accountant, Gene Jacobson. The IRS was interested in me. My corporate tax return had not been filed. This was the tax return for Harvey Martin Enterprises, through which came income from ventures like Dr. Pepper and the radio and TV commercials.

I got hold of a tax attorney, whose first reaction was that certain members of the Dallas branch of the IRS were bigoted and would love to make a case against a well-known black athlete. I retained the tax attorney to represent me, and he soon learned the IRS aimed for a fraud charge, saying I'd deliberately tried to defraud the U.S. government out of tax money.

"You could go to jail, Harvey," my lawyer said.

I date the start of four years of personal hell to the news I received in this telephone conversation. It was only after *four years* of worry and anxiety and tremendous amounts of money paid to my lawyers, that fraud charges were ultimately dropped.

I started feeling sorry for myself. I made my living at football, not as an accountant, and yet it seemed I'd have to pay for the mistake of an accountant. I worried myself sick about going to jail. Almost every day the lawyers reported that the IRS was threatening prosecution and criminal charges. There were so many meetings in the lawyers' office I began to think I lived there.

I couldn't doubt that the IRS wanted to nail me. Rumors spread all over Dallas: *Harvey Martin is in trouble.* Friends told me they'd been questioned about me by the IRS. My lawyer said he thought the IRS had tapped my phone. None of this helped my mental state.

The news on the football front didn't cheer me up either. Roger Staubach, having been knocked unconscious so many times during the 1979 season, sensibly announced his retirement. That meant Danny White would be our new quarterback, and I was worried about how the offense would function without Roger.

Still, I believed we'd be a team to reckon with. Our defense would be solid, which I knew to be the most important factor in winning football games. If offense made the crucial difference, Dan Fouts would be in the Super Bowl every year.

Danny White, son of U.S. Supreme Court Justice Byron "Whizzer" White, himself a football player of note, got drafted in the third round in 1974 out of Arizona State. Danny played backup quarterback to Roger for six years, and like Roger he thought, dressed, and acted conservatively. I doubted he could lead the Cowboys the way Roger had.

During the off-season I had obtained what I considered an important assignment from ABC: I'd be one of the announcers of the Superteams competition.

I believe an earlier get-together with Don Meredith and his wife, Susan, at Don's home in Beverly Hills helped me win the assignment. Meredith, Susan, and I went to dinner and saw actor Robert Conrad at a nearby table. I could sense Meredith's hostility to Conrad and figured I knew why. Conrad always played the tough guy, but Meredith knew what tough really meant—he'd played with Lilly and Jethro Pugh—and probably didn't like the airs he believed Conrad put on. As George Plimpton pointed out in *Paper Lion,* you really need to play pro football to understand how violent the game is, and many people who have played pro football can't help but be hostile toward individuals who only *pretend* they're tough.

I heard Meredith groan when he saw Conrad approaching our table. I shook hands with the actor, and we talked for a few minutes. He seemed a good enough guy to me.

"He's probably peeing in his pants," Meredith sneered when Conrad had left, "after meeting Harvey Martin."

Meredith gave me tips on what I needed to succeed as a TV announcer. He said I spoke well, a *sine qua non,* and taught me how to "work my eyes" and use my hands while on camera.

My assignment to the Superteams competition hardly constituted hazardous duty. Before going to Hawaii for the actual filming, ABC sent us to Freeport in the Bahamas to "practice." Reggie Jackson, another Superteams announcer, gave me a pointer.

"Be bland," Reggie advised.

Reggie, of course, was anything but bland, and I learned that nothing scared him. Reggie was so sure of himself, so confident of his abilities, that he felt he could tell anybody anything and not have to worry himself. He'd just start talking. You could take him or leave him—he didn't care. Most of the time a business advisor stayed close at his side, discussing deals.

Lynn Swann, another Superteams announcer, also showed me the ropes. Swann had sparkled against the Cowboys in two Super Bowls, but Sharon Bell assured me he was otherwise okay. Swann had previously dated Sharon's sister.

I spent a lot of time with Lynn and Reggie. Athletes socializing with each other isn't actually that common. After living through more than half a day with players, the last thing you want to do is see more players. A professional athlete may have two or three good friends who are teammates—in my case, Too Tall Jones, Billy Joe DuPree, and Drew—but groups of players rarely go out at night together.

There's another reason for this. Players don't want teammates knowing what they're doing. Many NFL players make a great deal of money during their peak years, but those years are few. They don't want to risk others' finding out something that might get them in trouble and jeopardize their careers. Say, in a friendly debate, a Dallas Cowboy bets the bartender $100 that the Vikings will defeat the Eagles. A teammate, overhearing this, would be in a position to cause the bettor a great deal of grief.

NFL players are told to be role models for kids, are expected to live in a fishbowl. Being human, they often fall short of expectations. Nobody's perfect. Justifiably or not, many athletes prefer to have non-athletes as friends. The public professed amazement when Cowboy players said they didn't know Thomas Henderson was addicted to drugs, but it couldn't have been any other way. Most players didn't *want* to know Thomas's business. *I* didn't know! That brings up another condition endemic to many players: They're so wrapped up in themselves—they have to be to perform at a world class level—that they often do not pay enough attention to people around them. Thus they are poor judges of character.

In Freeport I once again met the great David "Deacon" Jones, a Hall-of-Famer and a member of the old Rams Fearsome Foursome. Jones had been my first football hero; as a boy I'd loved watching him on TV. "Deacon," I said, as soon as I caught him alone, "I realize my teammate Bob Lilly is being inducted into the Hall of Fame this year, but I want you to know you've always been my favorite football player."

This giant man had possessed tremendous speed. He could run down plays on the other side of the field. Deacon's greeting to me was unusually warm, and later I heard something that made me feel almost as good as receiving the Super Bowl co-MVP award: Deacon's wife took me aside and said, "Harvey, Deacon thinks you're the best defensive end ever to play the game."

In Freeport Deacon was entered in the 100-yard dash and slated to go up against currently active players. He would be running against some real burners: wide receivers and running backs who had been sprinters and track stars. But I remembered Deacon chasing down quarterbacks from behind and thought maybe he had a chance.

"You got a chance?" I asked my hero.

"I'm gonna win, Harvey," he bubbled. "I tell you, boy, I'm gonna win."

I smiled like the cat who'd swallowed the canary, telling everyone who'd listen that my hero Deacon Jones was going to win the 100-yard dash. They looked at me as if I were crazy. *To hell with them*, I thought. *Wait till they see old Deac go.*

I glued my eyes to the start of the race. Deacon came blasting out of the blocks and actually had a lead at the 10-yard mark. Then he might as well have hit a wall. I never saw someone slow down so fast. The sprinters and wide receivers zipped by him, quickly opening up a huge lead.

But Deacon gutted it out, reeling across the finish line what seemed minutes after the others. I rushed up to him, microphone in hand.

"You're still my hero, Deacon," I said.

"I let you down, Harvey," he gasped.

"Hell, Deacon," I said honestly, "you beat 'em for ten yards, and that's all a defensive end ever has to do."

Reggie Jackson announced the baseball players competition in Hawaii, and I went with him to look for the best places from which to film. We walked to the top of a hill overlooking the high school practice facilities where the NFL players worked out. "Look at all of them," Reggie said. "There ain't a player out there whose whole salary equals what I make just from TV." A cloud passed over Reggie's face—"Well, maybe Franco." He turned to me. "And you, Harvey? How much do you make?"

That's how Reggie acted. Always saying what came to his mind at any moment. At that instant he worried I might be outdoing him financially. I didn't tell him he had no worry in that regard, that besides the IRS on my tail, I had numerous businesses that were shaky at best.

I looked at Reggie's shadow, the financial advisor in the three-piece suit, who was always at the baseball star's elbow, and felt a twinge of envy.

Reggie could have played football in the NFL. He'd been a star defensive player at Arizona State. Bo Jackson, the First of the First for the Tampa Bay Buccaneers, faced a decision similar to the one Reggie had to make.

Bo could be a star in either football or baseball. If he asked me which to choose, I would have told him to take the sport that gave him the most happiness. Evidently, choosing baseball, he did just that. The other two main considerations were longevity and money. The odds are he can play baseball longer; in football he might have suffered a career-ending injury on his first play from scrimmage. As the winner of the Heisman Trophy, he surely would have gotten more cash from football.

From Hawaii I flew to New York City to do voiceovers for the Superteams telecast, a job I excelled at because of my radio experience. But I thought I'd done well on TV, too.

I took the opportunity to sample more of New York City's night life. Many of the waiters and waitresses were talented out-of-work actors. I talked to them whenever I could about their careers in the theater. I thought I'd like to try acting.

New York City's night life was much more free-spirited than Dallas's. Too Tall, Henderson, and I virtually created night life in Dallas.

The football bad news, as I've said, was Roger's retirement. But the good news was Too Tall's return to the Cowboys. He'd gone undefeated in his year as a fighter, earning more than $300,000, an increase over his salary as a football player. Overjoyed at his return, calling him "my partner," I heartily shook his hand the first time I saw him after the announcement of his return. What had boxing been like? I asked him. "Tougher than football," he said. "You got no pads in the ring."

I knew Too Tall would also serve as an example to younger players that the Cowboys won games because of hard work and dedication. The young players needed to learn *how* to win. Well, they could learn from Too Tall, and from Randy White as well.

"You really coming back?" I said to Too Tall.

"Yeah. I can't throw an overhand right. Holmes and Cooney would kill me because of that."

As always, Too Tall saw plainly and clearly. He was a sane, even-headed man who didn't delude himself. He'd suffered a shoulder injury at Tennessee State—that was why he couldn't throw that overhand right.

The Cowboys had an area of the locker room called "the Ghetto." I liked to sit nearby and listen to the loud talk of Ron Springs, Tony Dorsett, Dennis Thurman, and Drew. You could always get the latest gossip from the Ghetto. One day the talk centered on the teammate who'd been eating at McDonald's with his girl friend when his wife drove up. The player spilled his food all over his shirt trying to hide under one of those tiny tables. To no avail.

His wife parked her car right next to his, went inside, glanced down at him, shook her head, went to the counter and placed her order.

"She didn't tell him, 'You deserve a break today'?" some wit asked.

"Nah," another answered. "But she didn't kill him either."

The fear that a wife would catch a player with a girl friend was a main locker room worry.

The Cowboys had plenty of characters playing for them through the years. Landry once decided to move Pete Gent from split end to flanker for a game against the Eagles. "You're going to play on the other side next week," Landry told him.

"I'm going to play for Philadelphia?" Gent asked.

Even the fans can be characters. Multimillionaire Danny Faulkner, with whom I once sat on a bank board, paid $1 million for a "sky box" on the 35-yard line of Texas Stadium.

Some of my favorite quotes appeared in *The Semi-Official Dallas Cowboys Haters' Handbook*:

"If Tom Landry and Bud Grant had a personality contest, nobody would win."

—DON MEREDITH

"I don't know. I only played there nine years."

—WALT GARRISON, when asked if
Tom Landry ever smiles

"Pittsburgh might have a little better team, but we've got two weeks to get ready. Give Landry two weeks and he'd have beaten Nazi Germany."

—Cowboy publicist DOUG TODD before
Super Bowl XIII

"Gentlemen, nothing funny ever happened on a football field."

—Tom Landry

In 1980 we added James Jones, a good north and south runner who I thought could earn us some playoff money. We also added Timmy Newsome from Winston-Salem State, a big, tough running back, who later left training camp because Landry moved him from that position to blocking back. Newsome didn't like to block.

When I heard that, I wondered, *What is this, a baby?* Were we running a nursery? He didn't like to block? Hell, I hadn't liked Art Shell's slugging me in the ribs with his fists, but I took it. Newsome later returned, but his kind of petulant behavior didn't bode well.

Another new player was defensive back Eric Hurt, who promptly got hurt. I could relate a hundred sad stories like his. Hurt had good speed, but he just didn't quite measure up. He always talked about coming back to the Cowboys when the injury healed, but he never did.

Being released by the team shattered Hurt so much that for a time he lived a lie. He went around town wearing a Cowboy shirt and saying he'd soon be back with the team. He wore a cast on his hand for four months. When I asked him about it, he broke down and told me the truth. He'd boasted about being a Cowboy, and when some guy said he wasn't, Hurt clobbered him and broke his hand. Hurt's problem as a football player was that he made mental errors, which in the case of a defensive back means you're giving up touchdowns, and no team can afford to do that. Still, many in Dallas thought Eric Hurt a hero. That's the way it is in my city, which loves its team. Even if you've only *tried out* for the Cowboys, you're a hero.

Usually I spent little time worrying about our offense. "To hell with those bumblers" was the attitude of many of our defensive players. But this year, with Roger gone, I had to worry.

First and foremost, how would Danny White do trying to fill the big shoes of Staubach?

I believed my fears justified. I saw Tony Hill quickly become White's favorite pass target, while Drew virtually disappeared from the offense.

What was this?

The pass receiver never lived who was Drew's superior. On tough third-down calls, when the defense looked for a pass and the receiver could expect to be clobbered, Danny did throw to Drew. But on the relatively easy first- and second-down passes, Danny went mostly to Hill. Hill didn't perform at his best with a defensive back right on him ready to deliver a damaging blow, whereas Drew would hang on to the ball even if Hollywood Henderson, Lawrence Taylor, and Dick Butkus hit him simultaneously.

Drew's lessened role in the offense began to eat him up inside, but he complained to only a few friends. He was a team player, and the last person to cause dissension.

I can't blame Danny White. After all, Tom Landry called all the plays from the sidelines, and Danny just followed orders.

Heading into the first regular season game against the Redskins on "Monday Night Football," I knew our defensive front four was rock-solid: Too Tall and I at ends, Randy White and former Baltimore Colts All-Pro John Dutton at tackles. The Redskins made a lot of noise about avenging their NFC East divisional championship defeat to us the year before, but I didn't care how much smoke they blew.

I was a Cowboy first, last, and always, which meant I didn't like Washington, our ultimate rival, and especially not Joe Theismann and John Riggins. The latter, a hard-drinking, overrated running back, surprised me not at all when later he got drunk at, of all places, the White House, and managed to insult U.S. Supreme Court Justice Sandra Day O'Connor—"Loosen up, Sandy baby," he said—

before passing out on the floor. But long before this I knew Riggins to be crude, even gross at times. It didn't explain why my dislike for him reached such intensity. Plenty of other players are crude. The bottom-line reason: I hated Riggins because he played for the Redskins.

Riggins, a Kansas country boy who made a lot of money—"I hope they pay me $900,000 next year to sit on the bench," he said, referring to the $800,000 he reportedly made in 1985 as a part-timer—couldn't even have started for the Cowboys, in my opinion. Certainly he had none of the dazzling moves, the lightning speed, or the great athletic skills of Tony Dorsett. What Riggins did have was The Hogs, a bunch of 300-pound offensive linemen who could move a brick wall forward a few yards. All Riggins had to do was get behind these behemoths and let them plow forward for him for a few yards each down. For this he deserved to be called a great player? For this he earned $800,000 a year?

The Redskins-Cowboys rivalry had started before the teams ever played a single down. George Preston Marshall, owner of the Redskins, had refused to vote to allow Clint Murchison to own the new franchise. But Murchison needed that vote. What could he do?

At the time, Marshall and his wife, Corinne, were in the middle of a divorce. Corinne had written the Washington fight song, "Hail to the Redskins." Behind Marshall's back, Murchison purchased the rights to the song.

"George," Murchison said over the phone, "are y'all plannin' to play the Redskins' fight song? Y'all know what I'm talkin' 'bout. 'Hail to the Redskins'?"

"Of course," replied the bewildered Marshall. "Yes."

"Nobody," snarled Murchison, "plays my fight song without my permission."

Marshall agreed to allow Murchison a franchise in exchange for being allowed to play the beloved fight song!

The Redskins-Cowboys rivalry was intense. John Wilbur said of Washington Coach George Allen: "George never used to say 'the Dallas Cowboys.' It was always 'the goddamned Dallas Cowboys.' " The rivalry extended to the Texas delegation to the United States House of Representatives trying to pass a resolution calling for a Dallas victory. It was expressed in things like Diron Talbert calling Roger Staubach "a pussy." Roger replied, "I knew Talbert hated quarterbacks who ran. So I'd run."

I had one goal going into that Monday night opener against the Skins, and I figured if I succeeded, we'd win the game. My goal was to put Joe Theismann in the hospital, but it almost worked out just the opposite. I came after him full-tilt, launching myself into a headlong dive, thinking I might decapitate him, but Larry Cole charged from the opposite side with the same thought in mind, and Theismann, sneaky little devil, ducked.

Cole and I smashed head-on into each other. I suffered a chipped bone over my left eye, and double vision for more than a week. If you can't see, you shouldn't play, but I did, the next week against Denver, and we got clobbered 41–20.

But in that Monday night opener, the Redskins, despite all their talk, didn't score a touchdown, and we won 17–3.

My injury, combined with my growing business and tax problems, made it increasingly difficult for me to concentrate on my Number One job, football. But somehow, digging deep, I succeeded. As always, I led the team in sacks.

The Cowboys posted a 12–4 record in 1980, but established what I considered a troublesome trend. Great teams are consistent. They average perhaps 30 points a game and in most games score close to their average.

The 1980 Cowboys weren't consistent. For example, one Sunday we clobbered the Forty-niners 59–14, and the very next week we lost to the Eagles 17–10. We'd scored 49 more points against one team than we had the next week against another.

The Sunday after the Eagles game we smashed the Chargers 42–31. Later in the season we defeated Washington again, 14–10, and the week after that ran over Seattle 51–7, a 37-point differential in our offensive production. Just two weeks after scoring 51 points against Seattle, we got buried by the Rams 38–14. All an individual needed to do to see something was wrong with the Cowboys was check the wide variances in the scores of our games. We weren't consistent.

The cause: our new quarterback, who couldn't on a game-by-game basis match the every-week excellence of Roger; and new offensive players who didn't understand that greatness in football involves doing it *every game, every down, first play to last.* Sometimes they waxed brilliant, but a brilliant football team does it *all the time.* Many of these were not players from our great teams of the 1970s that had fought the mighty Steelers down to the last second of a game we *should have* won for the right to be called Team of the Decade.

Too Tall came back better than ever. I believe boxing helped him; he'd become quicker and more agile than before. He'd discovered new parts of his body and ways to use them.

I had a particularly good game against St. Louis in the regular season. On one series I registered two sacks and a "hurry" on three consecutive plays. Just before this I'd been motivated by Cardinals offensive tackle Roger Finney, who pointed his finger at me to psych himself up but accomplished just the opposite. "You're mine, Harvey," he growled.

Ha! I ran *over* him three consecutive plays, and when they replaced him with a new guy, I ran over the new guy, too.

I developed a ritual for right after pregame warmups. I'd always be the last Cowboy off the field, and I'd walk over to where the opposition's offensive line worked out and stare nastily at each of them, especially my own man.

The day I knocked Roger Finney out of the game, the Cardinals looked at me as if I were crazy, applauded, and laughed at my pregame tough guy act. Not only did I blast Finney out of the game, I knocked quarterback Jim Hart out. I believe during my career Hart had to leave four different games against us because of injuries sustained by my hitting him. "I'm glad we're on the same team," he told me jokingly before a Pro Bowl. The trouble was, I also suffered numerous injuries because of my kamikaze charges at Hart, usually because when he ducked I'd run into somebody else.

We won our last game of the regular season 35–27 over the Eagles. The contest followed that humiliating 38–14 defeat by the Rams.

How's this for consistency? In the NFC wildcard playoff game we crushed those same Rams 34–13 to qualify for the divisional playoff against Atlanta. I would have thought us a better team if we'd defeated the Rams 30–21 in each game.

The Falcons, we knew, were one rough collection of studs. They had Steve Bartkowski, Lynn Caine, and workhorse running back William Andrews, who'd burned up the league in the 1980 season. I worried about Mike Kenn, reputedly a mean dude—a beach boy, muscle man, strong-guy all-America type. I watched Kenn on films till I got sick of his pretty face. When a sportswriter asked me what I thought of him, I said, "I can't wait to get my hands on the ****."

I had a *great* game against Atlanta, but we trailed 24–10 entering the fourth quarter. Robert Newhouse made it 24–17; then the Falcons kicked a field goal to lead 27–17 with 3:40 to go. Danny White, for one day, at least, an admirable fill-in for Roger, hit Drew Pearson to make it 27–24. And, as in so many dramatic comebacks, it was Drew who caught the game-winner, a brilliant grab between two Falcon defenders with just forty-nine seconds left.

I dominated men much bigger than myself, partly because of the state-of-the-art training ideas of the Cowboys, especially the fact drilled into us constantly that at the point of impact a lesser mass with greater speed can push around a larger mass going at a lower speed. I could run over bigger men because my speed, call it a factor of 10, multiplied by my weight, call it a factor of 5, came to a force of 50, while my opponent's speed might be a factor of 2, combined with a mass of 20, which multiplied to only 40.

We met the Eagles in Philadelphia on a bitterly cold day (three Philadelphia fans who painted themselves green and appeared naked from the waist up, nearly died in the freezing weather) and played miserably. The defense didn't play particularly well. Time and again we allowed ourselves to get hooked to the outside, allowing Wilbert Montgomery to run wild on the inside. The Eagles coaching staff had done an excellent job scouting us.

We lost 20–7, but though the defense didn't intimidate and overpower, as we'd hoped to, that's not why we came up short.

The offense didn't show a thing. Seven points? How many NFL teams can win scoring only 7 points? Despite Montgomery, despite being fooled on those inside runs, we gave up only 20 points, and any NFL team coached by the brilliantly innovative Tom Landry should score more than 20.

The loss to Philadelphia was a bitter pill, stopping us one step short of the Super Bowl. We had defeated this same Philadelphia team in the last regular season game 35–27. (Note the offensive inconsistency—35 points one game, 7 the next against the same bunch.)

The Oakland Raiders represented the AFC in Super Bowl XV. We defeated the Raiders in the regular season at the madhouse Oakland Coliseum, 19–13. Playing on a neutral field, I figured we could handle them with even greater ease.

But maybe not. We weren't consistent. We might kill Oakland. Or they might blow us out of the stadium.

Our offensive line missed Rayfield Wright, whom Landry had advised to retire. Rayfield had a bad leg, but I thought he performed better on one leg than most players on two. Rayfield was a rock. He, along with Blaine Nye, Ralph Neely, John Fitzgerald, and John Niland, typified what had made the Cowboys great. But from this group only Fitzgerald remained. The replacements for the others were great athletes, and the best of them, Pat Donovan, made All-Pro, as did Herb Scott, but they lacked a leader. Drew tried to provide that leadership, but young players need someone from their own age group to look up to. None of these talented offensive linemen could be called a leader, as Rayfield had been for his generation.

I thought nothing better illustrated how cruel pro football can be than the way Rayfield left the Cowboys. He'd just gotten a divorce and desperately needed money. I knew for a fact that he begged Tom Landry for one more year, but Landry wouldn't give it to him. In Landry's behalf, he believed it was in Rayfield's best interest not to risk further injury.

By any reckoning, however, Rayfield was treated shabbily. When Roger Staubach retired, the Cowboys called a big press conference to announce the event. But when Rayfield left, after protecting Roger for so many years, it was as if he'd never been with the team at all. In reality, Rayfield played on every Super Bowl team the Cowboys ever had, including the 1970 and 1971 versions, but no press conference trumpeted this great black star's exit from Dallas.

Toward the end of his career, Rayfield had to compete for his job with Andy Fredericks, a competent performer but not deserving even mention in the same breath with Rayfield. The many years Rayfield spent, brilliant but unheralded, in the trenches, should have earned him the security of knowing he would start, especially when the player the Cowboys said provided his competition had such vastly inferior skills.

When Landry told Rayfield he no longer wanted him on the team, perhaps he figured Rayfield was costing the team too much money. But how about all the money Rayfield made for the Cowboys playing in five Super Bowls? An NFL team demands loyalty but is not so quick to give it back.

And who's to know? Can those Cowboy computers gauge what's in a man's heart? Who's to say that if Rayfield had been given the one more year he pleaded for, he wouldn't have stabilized our inconsistent offensive line and led us to another Super Bowl triumph?

Any sensible assessment of our prospects for the coming season had to center on whether Danny White could win the big game. The Cowboys had always counted on Roger, and we didn't know if Danny could fill the bill.

I'm just a baby in the league.

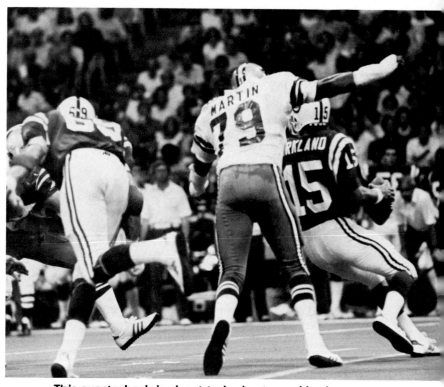

This quarterback is about to be hurt—real bad.

I got Craig Morton—then playing with the Giants—on this rush.

Overleaf:
Sacking Dan Pastorini of the Oilers

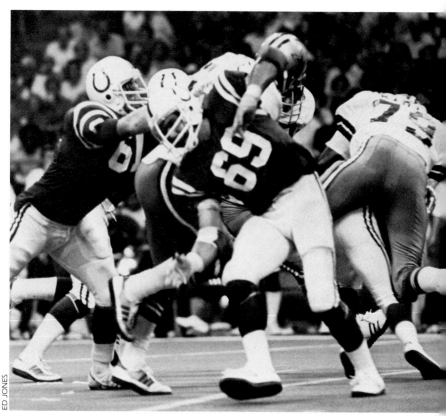

ED JONES

Clobbering Bert Jones of the Colts

With the cast of *Damn Yankees*

Injured after running into my own teammate Larry Cole in a Washington game

The 1981 rookies disappointed me in one respect—attitude. There was something out of sync with these young players, and the problem carried over into the following years. Take, for example, cornerback Rod Hill, our first-round draft choice in 1982. He had great speed and reflexes, but he tried to be one of the guys too quickly. He interrupted players like Tony Dorsett and Ron Springs while they conversed, butting right in. This violated an unwritten NFL protocol. To become one of the guys you first have to earn your way, but Hill stepped in as if he'd been with us in the wars with the Steelers.

When Tony Dorsett arrived on the team, we treated him like a rookie. The same happened to Charlie Waters, Drew Pearson, Roger, myself. We came to belong because of what we did. When the veterans told us to sing a song, we sang; when they sent us on errands to get pizza, we moved as quickly as if the order had come from Landry on the field.

The new rookies didn't like this. Somehow they figured they deserved to be treated like veterans right away.

I don't mean to sound like a cranky curmudgeon, but reasons exist for the tradition of a pecking order on football teams, just as they do in the army. For one thing, a rookie may not make it in the NFL. A case in point is none other than Rod Hill.

I watched in amazement as youngsters who had never started in an NFL game demanded to be the first on the team bus, took for granted the choice seats on a plane, and elbowed themselves to the front in the training room to get their legs taped. You might think those are all little things, but I believed they signaled that the Cowboys as a team were in trouble.

The rookies also went straight for the night life and the girls. True, I became one of the Cowboys' champions in these departments, but I waited until I'd secured my position on the team. Not the members of the new generation. Right after practice, while Randy White tried to finagle a game film he could watch at home, the rookies chattered about the conquests they'd made last night and the parties they were headed for that evening.

"It's like being at a damn hen party," mumbled Too Tall, showing his disdain for the gossip flying around the locker room.

Often dozens of women waited outside the practice field for the players. At least Too Tall and I went looking for girls, and only when we figured the football was over. But now it seemed a player's football life ended with the official practice, and they didn't feel compelled to expend any further effort.

As always, in 1981 there were players missing from Thousand Oaks whom I had come to think would always be with the Cowboys. Larry Cole, for example, had just retired. This hard-nosed, intelligent defensive lineman fit perfectly into the Cowboy system. He wouldn't have been a star anywhere else, but he was with the Cowboys because Landry's system relied so much on brains. Many of the Cowboys had good minds. Blaine Nye (whom we called Doctor Blaine) spent his time getting university degrees. Larry Cole worked at becoming a real estate whiz in a booming Dallas market. He had his life beautifully compartmentalized, something I wished I could say for myself.

We called Larry Cole "the Dean," a title he won by becoming the oldest Cowboy in terms of years of service.

I felt it a great honor when I later became the Dean, the youngest in Cowboy history. Jethro Pugh and Bob Lilly held the title before me; now it belongs to Too Tall.

As the Dean and spokesperson for the defensive line, I arranged a pact among ourselves against our offensive line. We decided to go out and kick their asses every day in practice, which served a twofold purpose: First, we wanted to shake them up, pound them out of their lethargy; second, in our own self-interest, we didn't want to do all the work on Sundays. We were sick of having to drag our bodies back on the field every week to endure more pain and seeing the effort go to waste.

I thought our action unprecedented. No one would even have conceived of doing this against Rayfield and Neely.

"If we gotta toughen them up," I said, "then that's what we'll do."

We took it easy on Pat Donovan. Pat always worked hard and didn't deserve our rough tactics. Some members of the offensive line complained—"Hey, man, lay off!"—and when that didn't stop us, they claimed they could get hurt in practice. That didn't work either. We figured, better *they* get hurt in practice than *we* get hurt by losing on Sunday.

I liked rookie defensive lineman Don Smerek from the start. And so did Coach Ernie Stautner. (Stautner, incidentally, while playing for the Steelers, had broken the nose of New York Giants quarterback Tom Landry in a 1952 NFL game.) Smerek worked as hard as anybody, always had a positive attitude, and quietly fit right in. I enjoyed drinking beer with Smerek, who had an excellent repertoire of jokes. Unlike Rod Hill, he didn't interrupt Too Tall to tell them. Smerek got hurt early in training camp, which for most rookies would have been the death knell, but Stautner kept him on the team.

To repeat, because it can't be emphasized enough, the problem we faced was players who'd seen the Cowboys win so often on TV that they thought it was automatic, never understanding that we got to those Super Bowls because we busted our balls. The wonderful Dallas fans treated these rookies very well, but as the praise went to their heads, the rookies didn't realize that it was people like Too Tall and Rayfield who had earned this treatment *for* them.

All this aside, the Cowboys still had a very good team in 1981. But the part of the team that needed help the least got the most: the defense. We added two absolutely marvelous rookies who, along with the rest of the defensive backfield, became known as "Charlie's Angels," in honor of our star defender Charlie Waters.

One of them, Everson Walls, introduced himself to me early in training camp. I had a razor in my hand and shaving cream on my face. He stuck out his hand and said cheerfully, "I'm from Grambling."

"What'd you play?" I asked.

"Defensive back."

"You any good?"

"I led the country last year in intercepts," he said, without a trace of braggadoccio. He just stated a fact.

"When were you drafted?"

"I wasn't. I'm a free agent."

"Where you from?"

"Dallas. Hamilton Park."

"Yeah?" I said noncommittally. But I promised myself to keep an eye on this boy from Grambling who led the nation in intercepts.

It didn't take me long to see that Everson Walls had the best move on the ball of anyone I'd ever watched, including all-time great Mel Renfro, who rightly is enshrined in the Cowboy Ring of Honor (the highest honor the Cowboys bestow, your name forever on a deck of Texas Stadium—the equivalent of the monuments in Yankee Stadium honoring Babe Ruth and Lou Gehrig). Walls brought additional zip to our defense, caused turnovers, generally made life miserable for opposing offenses. How did Everson do his rookie year? He led the *league* in interceptions. I saw right away that Everson had fire in his eyes, hunger, that he'd make our ball club or die trying. Our other sensational rookie defensive back was Michael Downs. But I didn't have to ask Michael where he attended school. He went to South Oak Cliff High School, where he played for Coach Jett, and then on to Rice University, where he made All-Southwest Conference. Michael never said much, but he hit everything that moved.

"Homeboy!" I'd shout when Michael smashed down a running back. "That's my homeboy!"

Michael Downs knew all the Harvey Martin stories. It surprised and honored me to learn that Coach Jett used my history to inspire his teams. It went like this: "If big, ugly, clumsy, scared-out-of-his-pants Harvey Martin can become All-Pro, just think what you guys can do!"

Sadly, our great old pro Preston Pearson, a fourteen-year NFL veteran, was gone. Everyone on the team had looked up to Preston, knew that on key third-down plays he'd come up with the crucial catch. Preston was a pro's pro and, despite those fourteen tough years in the NFL, still had the physique of a twenty-five-year-old. He consistently tested as having less body fat than any other player on the team. In my opinion, it was another case of the Cowboys giving up too early on a valuable veteran.

In 1981 I again led the Cowboys in sacks, but mentally it required an almost superhuman effort. In my business dealings, we'd expanded to five barbecue restaurants, and they were in trouble. We got plenty of good publicity, however, by bringing ribs to the training field after practice on Thursdays, and we acquired a booth at the prestigious Texas State Fair, where much of Texas saw us right next to Fletcher's Corn Dogs, perhaps the single most popular booth.

To continue to finance Smokey John's, we took out a $150,000 loan from an investor who insisted I take out a $150,000 life insurance policy to guarantee repayment.

The entire episode with the barbecue restaurants proved I didn't have time to devote the effort required to oversee so many varying enterprises. My naïveté made me think I could drum business into the restaurants, then sit back and enjoy the profits. Instead I began to drown in red ink from Smokey John's and in worry about the IRS, which almost daily threatened to indict me on criminal charges.

The problem with the Smokey John's in Oak Cliff was that the price of beef rose rapidly in the first (recession) year of the Reagan administration, and minority residents in Oak Cliff couldn't afford what we had to charge.

I blamed my partner; he blamed me. My attitude had been, "I'll get 'em in, you keep 'em in." That didn't cut the ice. When we ran specials, we packed the place, but at other times we didn't do enough business.

And I had other problems. Recipe's had become history. We'd experienced a constant turnover in managers, and our superb chef, the reason we had opened the restaurant in the first place, simply vanished. The quality of food went down, and so did the business. I counted myself lucky all I had to do was pay off a $10,000 note and watch the place go downhill.

During the 1981 off-season, I took a trip to San Francisco and made a semi-commitment to marriage: I gave Sharon Bell a $20,000 diamond engagement ring, and she agreed to marry me. I didn't set a date for the wedding, and Sharon warned, "Harvey, you're going to have to settle down, or there won't be any wedding and I'm not going to see you again."

I told Sharon she could return to Dallas with me, but she said she'd only do that as my wife. I foolishly breathed a sigh of relief. One part of me wanted to marry Sharon and settle down, but the other part still enjoyed the parties and the endless stream of women in and out of my Dallas home.

The Cowboys had another 12–4 season in 1981 and

won the NFC East. The highlights of the season for me were two more victories over the Redskins with Riggins and Theismann. But again we showed inconsistency, losing to the Forty-niners one week 45–14 (we'd defeated them the year before, 59–14), then coming back the next Sunday to smash the Rams 29–17.

Our offense got worse while our defense got better. In the 1980 regular season we scored 454 points; in 1981 we scored 358, almost 100 fewer. In 1980 we allowed 311 points, a figure we reduced to 270 in 1981.

Mom grew very worried about me in 1981. She could see that to save my financial hide, the Cowboys literally *had* to win. I depended on playoff money to keep me from financial disaster. I really had plunged in over my head. I became too busy putting out fires from the past to see the even bigger conflagration looming up ahead. It's good to put your eggs in a basket, but afterward you need to watch the basket. I simply didn't have time to do so and still play up to All-Pro expectations.

We crushed Tampa Bay in the divisional playoff 38–0, mainly because we stopped their great quarterback Doug Williams, who could throw a football 50 yards even with an opponent draped over his shoulders. I thought Williams physically and mentally the toughest quarterback I ever faced. I hit him hard enough to turn him into Silly Putty; he got back up, brushed himself off, and continued doing his job. Just charging past quarterbacks and saying, "I'm getting close," often struck terror into their hearts, but not Doug Williams.

A lot of players use words to intimidate or to make you angry. They curse you, call you the vilest names. Insulting someone's mother is supposed to be a no-no, although Mark May of the Redskins once told Randy White as they lined up opposite each other, "Tell your mother to come back to my hotel room tonight; we didn't finish last night, and she was great."

I gave Doug Williams a terrific pounding, but instead of

congratulations, it earned me derision from some of my black friends. "You never hit a white quarterback that hard," one of them said. I could have told him to call Joe Namath, Joe Theismann, or Jim Hart, but I let the matter go.

Against Tampa Bay, an inferior playoff team, the defense tried to deliver a message not to Doug Williams, but to Joe Montana, whom we figured we'd face for the NFC championship and the right to go to the Super Bowl. We wanted Montana to see us pound Williams and draw his own conclusions. But the young San Francisco quarterback didn't scare.

The Forty-niners game turned into a furious affair that we lost in the final seconds. Leading 27–21, we chased Joe Montana out of the pocket, and I swear he threw the ball away—but he threw it away to wide receiver Dwight Clark, who just happened to be there and just happened to make one of the most famous catches in the history of football, defeating us 28–27.

I shouldered part of the blame for the defeat. In my zeal to tear somebody apart and stop the other team's offense during the last drive, I overpursued a Forty-niner runner, who handed the ball back to Freddy Solomon running in the opposite direction. Solomon danced 30 yards down my side of the field.

I wasn't the only culprit on the play. Linebacker Guy Brown, also overenthusiastic, didn't maintain proper containment.

I smashed Montana numerous times that day, but he performed superbly under pressure, never losing his cool. When he threw that touchdown pass, I came to a stop and hoped the grounds keepers would dig a hole where I stood and bury me on the field.

I know this loss ranks with the hardest Coach Landry ever swallowed. Before we took the field, I could see him almost *willing* us to win.

I felt terrible on the plane trip back to Dallas, depressed not just by the loss but by knowing that many of my teammates wouldn't be back next year. Guys with big hearts were leaving, including D. D. Lewis, who announced this was his last game.

One D. D. Lewis story always made me laugh. When the Cowboys flew into St. Louis, he caught a glimpse of the famed Gateway Arch. "I didn't know St. Louis was the national headquarters of McDonald's," he wisecracked.

D. D. Lewis came up the hard way. Arrested and jailed at age thirteen for stealing a car, and forced to wash dishes in ninth grade to help support his family, he qualified as one of those individuals coaches talk about when they say football can prove a youngster's salvation.

D. D. told how as a rookie he'd received and accepted good advice from an experienced pro player:

We were playing the Green Bay Packers, and I had the opportunity to talk with Ray Nitschke. I told him that I was surprised that there were so few team drills in training camp, that almost everything we had been doing was individual, one-on-one sort of things. He told me that it was going to be the same when I got back to camp, that those were the kind of drills you had to prove yourself at. He told me that he made the Packers by knocking people around and then excelling on the specialty teams once the exhibition games began.

Man, I went back to Thousand Oaks and went nuts. I played like a wild man, doing everything I could think of to gain the coaches' attention.

Charlie Waters was also leaving. He was a good friend and a good family man. I'd been with Charlie when he first met his wife, Rosie.

Charlie had guts: I saw him play with a knee brace on each leg—and I couldn't stand to use even one. Charlie suffered a compound fracture of the left arm that required *four* operations and the implantation of a steel rod, but he came back from that, just as he did from knee surgery.

We thought of Charlie as another coach on the field. In fact, if he thought the coaches were wrong, he'd argue with them about coverages. Well, I thought, he'd left us quite an inheritance. I knew Charlie's Angels—Michael Downs and Everson Walls—would be around a long time.

On the plane flight home I tried to console Everson, but experience taught me that after such a defeat comforting words didn't exist.

San Francisco defeated Cincinnati in the Super Bowl. We would have defeated Cincinnati in the Super Bowl, too, a realization that made matters worse. Two years in a row now we'd lost the game that should have landed us in the world championship.

I thought about some of the younger players on our team, men who ran faster than Charlie, reacted quicker than D.D., had more strength than Jethro. But they weren't as good.

Physically I felt fine, although my speed in the 40 had diminished from 4:7 to 4:9. My experience more than made up for this slight loss in speed, and I still could run faster than almost any quarterback in the league.

Inevitably, I wondered how many years I had left to play. My future seemed bleak. My businesses were in deep trouble. *You've always had lots of hustle and enthusiasm*, I thought, *but you've never been too smart.*

felt a creeping despair early in 1982. I had a load of personal problems, and my businesses lay in shambles. It seemed to me that in trying to put something together for the future, I'd ruined the present. I'd simply tried to do too many things at once. I wondered how I'd even found the time to make mistakes in so many areas. The present looked dismal, and the future loomed worse. I worried constantly about what would happen to me.

It didn't take special insight to see that white players generally fared better than blacks when their playing days ended. And given my past record, I couldn't be optimistic about joining the small band of blacks (Pettis Norman, Preston Pearson, and a few others) who had succeeded in some other pursuit when they retired from the game.

I don't believe blacks are discriminated against in the NFL while they're playing—certainly not by Tom Landry, who always put the best player in the game, no matter what his color. Landry saw only talent. He put up with Thomas Henderson longer than any other coach would have because of Thomas's tremendous talent.

An NFL team's pay for the black athlete is commensurate with that for the white player. The problem comes when playing days end. After nine years in the NFL, I had to be particularly concerned about that. It was after football when the white player usually pulled far ahead of the black.

I couldn't think of many black ex-teammates who had set the world on fire. Most of the whites did fine, and I applauded them. I saw Charlie Waters on Lite beer commercials, and Roger Staubach and D. D. Lewis became highly successful businessmen in Dallas. Bob Lilly did TV commercials.

But I never saw Jethro Pugh selling a product on the screen. Walt Garrison made a good living doing TV ads, playing a tough guy (Walt was tough, all right), but how about Rayfield? Rayfield was a real tough guy. He could have broken Walt Garrison in half. The simple truth was that blacks didn't generally blend into the Dallas community after they left the game.

I found myself in a Catch 22 situation. I couldn't afford lawyers, but if I didn't pay a brigade of lawyers, I'd be in worse trouble than I already found myself. The IRS menaced me, and so did a veritable army of creditors. I had partners in all my business ventures, but since I was the one who made money, the creditors always came after me.

Worry became my constant companion. Since joining the Cowboys I'd always been outgoing and upbeat, accessible to everyone, but I didn't feel that way anymore. I couldn't even draw pleasure remembering some of our great triumphs on the field. I imagined a dagger raised, ready to plunge into my heart.

That year I worked as a sports reporter for Channel 5, the NBC affiliate in Dallas, and gained more valuable TV experience. On Mondays and Fridays I did live reports. I taped shows from nightclubs where the players hung out. A few I taped from my home. Tony Dorsett, John Dutton, Butch Johnson, and Ron Springs came to the clubs for interviews. No Cowboy ever turned me down for an interview, a big plus in football-crazy Dallas. I helped the Channel 5 ratings go up.

The players union called a strike in 1982 after the second game of the season, and I covered the strike for Channel 5. This time I stood 100 percent behind the players union, although I had to be careful what I said on the air.

My reasons for supporting the strike weren't wholly selfish, although I had a big personal stake. What primarily interested me was the issue of severance pay: the player receiving money when he retired or got released, based on the number of years he'd played. I had to think about such things.

The severance pay would help future Rayfields, who virtually in a single instant go from the top of the mountain to the depth of the valley. Severance pay would give the veteran player a chance. When he's through, physically and mentally exhausted, his body having absorbed a terrible beating, he needs more than a pat on the back and a coach telling a roomful of reporters how good he was. Some guys have never done anything but play football, starting in PeeWee League and going all the way through the NFL, and they need something they can count on while they adjust to a new life.

The strike shortened the 1982 season to nine games— eight were cancelled—and the Cowboys went 6–3.

During much of 1982 I thought I'd go crazy. I couldn't sleep. I had twenty lawsuits coming at me at one time, and I experienced fear every time I heard the phone ring. My legal bill was enormous, a Mount Everest in my mind, and I began going out to nightclubs *more* just to avoid the pressure than for any other reason. Time and again there'd be three signatures on one bank note, but the bank would come after *me* for the whole thing. I could understand the bank's point of view, but understanding didn't help.

Worst of all, I'd tried never to hurt anyone in business,

and now it seemed like I'd hurt everyone. At times I'd show up for practice without any sleep at all, running on pure adrenaline, my own great energy. My mind turned into scrambled eggs.

Al Lavan, a black Cowboy coach, noticed my zombie state and pulled me aside. Al was a hard worker, a good guy. "Harvey," he said, "you're not applying yourself. Why don't you just forget everything and be Harvey again?"

I flared into hostility. "You want me to be Johnny Jock!" I yelled. "I've been going through hell. You know it; the Cowboys know it. But no one has ever offered to help!"

Lavan was a decent man and he didn't deserve my getting hot with him. But I wallowed in self-pity. I'd been raised by my mom to think everybody was nice, but I found out some people actually got up in the morning intending to burn you. Several of my businesses had gone belly-up because I'd been stolen blind. Then there'd been the sapphire deal . . . and dozens of other rough situations.

I'd never tried to cheat anybody. I'd always been open and friendly. I'd put up with more drunken crap from fans than any ten other players, always lent a sympathetic ear to teammates, worked my guts out on the field. And all it brought me was disaster. This self-pitying, no-win way of thinking lasted perhaps a week, then I took Al Lavan's advice and began a frenzied series of workouts. By the time training camp arrived, I was ready to go. I thanked God my body and athletic skills hadn't deserted me.

In training camp came the worst blow of all. Gil Brandt and Tex Schramm walked out onto the practice field and waved at me to come over.

"Your name has just been mentioned in connection with a major cocaine bust in Dallas," Brandt said.

"*What!*" I was amazed, crestfallen. My heart sank to the pit of my stomach. *Oh God, no,* I thought.

"Do you know Danny Stone?" Brandt asked.

"Yes."

"Well, he's been arrested for dealing cocaine. He mentioned your name. We thought you needed to know."

I'd met Danny Stone in a nightclub. He was a hairdresser who knew a number of the Cowboys, and struck me as an individual who loved to be around football players. He bragged to me that he sold cocaine, and he always had some with him, using it to impress girls he met at the clubs. I never bought any cocaine from him, but on occasion I did use some, during a period starting in 1980 when my businesses began to crumble.

No excuse justifies the use of this terribly debilitating and addictive drug. I used it because I hoped it would provide relief from my problems, but it only made them worse.

The last time I'd talked to Danny Stone was when he'd called me two weeks before I came to training camp in 1982. Danny mentioned that he'd just returned from Miami, a reference I imagine he intended to impress me with, because he always boasted about what a big-time dealer he was. I knew he was small potatoes. The important thing about that phone call was that Danny made it from "Snow White's" house, and Snow White was a big-time dealer. Snow White's phone also was tapped. When drug agents raided Danny Stone's home, they found pictures he had taken of me and some girl friends at functions that he also attended.

The press began calling Snow White and Danny Stone the biggest cocaine dealers in Dallas. Snow White may have been, but Danny was mainly guilty of a running mouth. He bragged himself right into the penitentiary. Although it hadn't yet been made public, Tony Dorsett had been mentioned as having some connection with Snow White, whom I had never met or heard of.

Mom called me the next day. "Who are the two Cowboys who are supposed to be using cocaine?" she asked. "Do you know?"

"No ma'am," I lied.

I could count on the fingers of one hand the number of times I'd ever lied to my mother.

I did my Channel 5 show that night, and rumors spread like wildfire over the Thousand Oaks training camp. The players wondered which two of their teammates knew these guys. Schramm and Brandt knew but weren't talking.

The drugs I'd used had been alcohol, Percodan, marijuana, and cocaine. As I've said, I started using cocaine in 1980, the first time being with Danny Stone. It had been a spur-of-the-moment action: *What the hell,* I told myself, thinking, minute by minute, *If it makes me feel good, relieves the pressure, then do it.*

When the team arrived back in Dallas from Thousand Oaks, I found myself greeted by Doug Todd, the Cowboys' public relations director. "Have you seen this article?" he asked.

The article said both Dorsett and I were "implicated" as knowing cocaine dealers.

Mom was at the airport. She fought her way through the crowd to throw her arms around me. I knew if everything else collapsed, she'd always be in my corner. My lawyer also showed up, and a passel of reporters. "Don't say a word," said the lawyer.

There was only one thing left for me: what I always did best, football, and I made four sacks in the two regular season games played before the strike intervened.

During the strike period I thought the city of Dallas had forgiven. Wherever I went, people wished me well, acting as if my name had never made those ugly headlines. I spent a lot of time at the Memphis Restaurant and Bar on Belt Line Road in Addison during the strike. The place, now extremely popular, stood virtually empty at this time. I'd sit and read the newspaper, eat soup, and talk football.

In 1982 place-kicker Rafael Septien was told he suffered a "pulled groin." When the season ended, Rafael was told he needed surgery to repair a hernia.

Why wasn't he told earlier?

"You tell him and he worries," said a Cowboy official. "And he doesn't kick well. We just didn't tell him."

I was headed for my own critical moment with the Cowboy medical establishment. However, before that happened, in 1982, linebacker Anthony Dickerson suffered what also got diagnosed as a "groin pull." It turned out to be a separation of the pelvis.

My business problems continued to mount, and things just *seemed* better during the strike because my name and cocaine weren't continually being linked in the press. All that would end when Danny Stone and Snow White went on trial.

Investments I'd made in El Paso and San Antonio turned sour, and all of the Smokey's restaurants, except one, collapsed.

Ronald Reagan had hurt me when his agricultural policies caused an increase in the cost of beef, but now he helped me. A new bankruptcy law he'd gotten passed went into effect, and I took advantage of its provisions. I lost almost everything I had—Smokey's alone amounted to $500,000 worth of problems—but I came out better than I expected. I managed to keep my house and was freed of a mountain of debt.

I timed the bankruptcy perfectly. The day after it went into effect, the players union signed a new agreement guaranteeing severance pay, and this combined with my salary gave me a $340,000 cushion.

The situation caused a U.S. congressman to complain from the floor of the House of Representatives that Ronald Reagan's policies were so absurd that "a football player goes into bankruptcy one day and the next day has $340,000."

The congressman was right, but I rationalized that I

was only obeying the law of the land. My lawyers assured me my case was minor compared to what many truly big fish were doing. In any event, I celebrated the next day by buying my Mom a Cadillac.

We won our first two games after the strike ended, and it was the following week that I declared bankruptcy. Our next game pitted us against the Redskins in RFK. Although I hardly expected a friendly greeting from the Washington faithful, nothing—and I mean *nothing*—prepared me for what awaited.

I came onto the field to the loudest booing I've ever heard—a wall of boos, catcalls, and curses—and drunken Redskin fans showered me with pennies, their way of contributing to the easing of my financial woes. *Fuck you,* I thought. I walked out to the center of the field and held my head up, standing tall. I figured I was still a mean sonofabitch and could take anything they had to offer. *I made you so and so's cry plenty of times,* I thought. *Have your fun while you can.*

They did. They rode me mercilessly.

The Redskins' tackle Mark May, who'd told Randy White he'd slept with Randy's mother the night before, stood up right before the Redskins kicked an extra point. "Hey, Harvey," he jeered, "you want me to loan you some money?"

But we took care of business. Theismann, whom I hated, threw an interception, then turned his head to curse. I never gave him a chance. Before he could open his mouth, I slugged him under the chin and knocked him cold. Then I went completely crazy. I took after All-Pro wide receiver Art Monk and put him on his knees with a series of hard punches.

The ever-alert officials didn't see any of this. But NFL Commissioner Pete Rozelle did, when he watched game films the following week. He fined me $1,500, which was cheap enough considering what I'd done to Theismann and Monk.

Rozelle did something else I didn't care for. He took a sack away from me, which ended up costing me the NFL sack lead to Dennis Hairston. Hairston beat me for the sack championship this year. Regardless, I got named All-Pro.

Remarkably, I didn't get elected into the Pro Bowl. The players decide who goes to the Pro Bowl, and many of them simply didn't like me. My own teammates did, though, and that's what counted.

Perhaps I did carry my go-for-broke style of play too far on occasion. Once Tom Dempsey of the Eagles, who is handicapped (he's missing part of his right foot), blew a field goal against us, and one of our backs started to run the kick back. In his frustration, Dempsey took a kick at me. I swung around and decked him, which earned me dirty looks, shakes of the head, and laughter from my own teammates (mostly from defensive players)—Harvey, the guy who'll hit a handicapped person. I didn't bother to explain that Dempsey, handicapped or not, is a helluva tough, mean individual. Besides, he'd tried to kick me.

During games I often got carried away when shouting encouragement to our offense. I didn't use the cleanest language—Roger was the only man on our team who ever said "shucks"—and my positioning on the sidelines wasn't always by design. When a shower of expletives streamed from my mouth, I'd inevitably be standing right behind Coach Landry. He *never* turned around. I don't think he wanted to confirm who was employing the gutter language.

It should be clear that the Dallas Cowboys, on occasion called the Dallas Corporates, had far too many characters throughout the years to fit the simon-pure image of America's team: Lance Rentzel, caught "flashing" in front of a little girl and quickly traded to the Los Angeles Rams; Duane Thomas (nicknamed "The Sphinx" because he wouldn't talk to reporters), a gifted runner who quoted Shakespeare and called Landry "Plastic Man," and is remembered for asking, about the Super Bowl, "If it's the ultimate game, why are they playing it again next year?"; and Don Meredith, whose nose got broken *fourteen* times playing for the Cowboys, who said, quite sensibly, "The higher you climb the flagpole, the more people see your rear end."

I never met Cowboy defensive back Otto Brown, but he must have been something—my kind of guy. When players wanted to leave tickets for relatives and friends, they had them put in "will call." "This dude Will Call," Brown marveled. "He must be one popular stud. Almost everybody on the team gives him tickets."

My final break with Sharon Bell came during the 1982 season. She demanded that I set a definite date for our marriage or she'd call the whole thing off. I refused.

I believe my motives were good, but who can ever be absolutely sure why he acts? I told myself I was doing Sharon a favor, that a ton of garbage—the bankruptcy, the upcoming cocaine trial of Danny Stone—faced me, and she shouldn't have to go through all of it. I told her that I just couldn't set a definite date and she said, "I'm sorry, Harvey. I can't wait any longer. I hope you have a happy rest of your life."

I've always felt I was the ultimate loser with Sharon. Many times I've wished that I had set that date.

When the playoffs started, so did the cocaine trial of Snow White and Danny Stone. But from reading the papers you would have thought Tony Dorsett and I were being tried. Attempting to do his best for his client, Stone's lawyer mentioned my name as often as he could, hoping the jury would forget who was really in the dock.

Tony and I made headlines that just humiliated me. When Danny Stone testified that I'd used cocaine with him in 1980, which was true enough, the embarrassment sent me into a panic. It didn't ease my frenzied state of mind when he added that he didn't believe I'd ever used the drug before.

Three days before Round Two of the Super Bowl playoffs, against Green Bay, I called Mom and told her I was quitting football.

That night about midnight I went to see Rayfield Wright. "Just looking at Harvey," Rayfield later said, "I got chill bumps all over."

"I'm quitting," I said.

"Man, you gonna quit because of *that*?" said Rayfield, a man I'd never seen give up.

"I'm tired of fighting."

"Man, life *is* a fight. No matter how weak or tired you get, living *is* fighting."

I began to cry. No matter what Rayfield said, I couldn't be consoled. He correctly judged that more than anything else, I felt badly for my mom and what those headlines did to her.

Later in the morning I called my friend Billy Joe DuPree. But Billy Joe couldn't make the decision for me either.

I called Ernie Stautner, told him I was quitting, and hung up.

That morning I missed practice, an act unprecedented in my career. I sat alone at home, sunk in despair, and listened to the phone ring and ring. I later learned that Ernie Stautner called my house all morning. So did my mother. When I finally did pick up the receiver, it was my sister, Mary, on the other end.

I told Mary I wanted to go back to Mabank. I longed to return to my impenetrable cocoon and the innocent days of youth in east Texas: picking peas, fishing, hunting squirrel and rabbit, and dreaming of what I would make of my life. Mary chewed me out good. It brought back to mind a side of my childhood I'd forgotten: not fighting my own battles and my sister urging me to stand on my own two feet.

"He wanted to escape back to his old haven," Mary told a sympathetic *Sports Illustrated* reporter. "I lit into him. I told him I was going to leave my kids and sit on his front step until he went to practice."

"I can't take any more!" I yelled at my sister. Then I told her I was sorry.

"There you go again," Mary said to me sharply, "apologizing to everybody for showing your *real* feelings."

With Mary's words ringing in my ears, I trudged back to the Cowboys to do my best.

Randy White, a good friend and a great player, turned out to be one of the few Cowboys who proved to be supportive. Drew Pearson, on the other hand, voiced a more common attitude. "Hey," said Drew, "when we're talking drugs, it's stay as far away as possible. Guys have to do that just to protect themselves."

Maybe so, but it points out again what an outstanding year I had despite nerve-wracking, adverse circumstances. Not only did I make All-Pro, but I barely missed the sack championship. All this with very little support from friends and teammates.

I refused to stay hidden in my house. Along with Buddy Gregory, a Dallas businessman and good friend who stuck with me through thick and thin, I went out to the old nightclubs, heard the whispering, saw the fingers pointing, and sipped beer and held my head high.

In Round One of the Super Bowl Tournament, so named because of the strike-shortened season, we crushed Tampa Bay 30–17. In Round Two, which took place right after my brief "retirement," we cruised by Green Bay 37–26. I didn't play well against the Packers. During the Green Bay game and the subsequent NFC championship against the Redskins, all the off-the-field disasters caught up with me and marred my concentration.

We lost to the Redskins 31–17, but my inferior performance didn't make the difference.

When a team consistently comes close to capturing the

ultimate championship and falls short each time, it is not by accident. *Three straight years* we fought our way to the NFC championship game and each time got turned away. Great teams do *not* consistently lose the close game.

Losing three straight NFC championship games was unprecedented. Coach Landry said, "You'd think we'd have won one just by accident," but he knew better than anyone else that wasn't true. The chemistry we'd always possessed in the 1970s was missing from the Cowboys.

The Redskins, of course, won the Super Bowl, defeating the outgunned Miami Dolphins (who started young David Woodley at quarterback), and though I always cheered for the NFC entrant, it just made our loss to the Redskins hurt all the more. The Redskins defeated the Dolphins; in the regular season we'd easily defeated the Redskins, 24–10; ergo, we would have defeated the Dolphins *if* we'd qualified for the Super Bowl.

But as I said before about a different season, maybe not.

During the 1980s we had defeated two of the three previous Super Bowl champions during the regular season: Oakland and the Redskins. The other champion, the Forty-niners, we lost to by a *single point,* and only then on Dwight Clark's miracle catch.

The Cowboys of the 1980s had a serious flaw, maybe several of them, which would become glaringly obvious to me in 1983—my last year in the NFL.

14

My greatest desire during the 1983 off-season was to see my life return to a semblance of normalcy. Mentally debilitated, my blood pressure edging into the danger zone, every day dreading the arrival of the morning paper, I perceived a slender thread of hope and clung to it like a man drowning. The cocaine trial of Snow White and Danny Stone had ended with convictions for both. I prayed the matter would now be put to rest.

I began working out, making myself a promise to show up at training camp in the best condition of my career. I still had plenty of great football left in me.

But nothing improved. Even as a rookie I'd been able to make lots of appearances—talking to kids, promoting products, and speaking at various functions. Now nobody wanted me. A stigma attached to me that I appeared powerless to shed.

I didn't even get invited to parties. Except for my friend Buddy Gregory and a few others, no one but my family bothered to call. Michael and Sydney Schutze, who knew how lonely I'd become, had me over to their home every Wednesday for dinner and "Dynasty." But mostly I got treated like a leper, like someone carrying a contagious disease.

Instead of with references to Super Bowls, championship teams, sacks, and All-Pro, my name continually
appeared in sentences that included the word *cocaine*.
Though never charged with any crime, I was treated like a
criminal, a pariah, a bad person for decent folks to be
around. Now a thoroughly outgoing adult, I found myself
being forced back to the introversion of my childhood.

I received one piece of good news: The IRS dropped
its fraud charges. A trustee for the bankruptcy court
suggested I sue the IRS for unfair treatment, but the last
thing I wanted or needed was more hassle. A fight with the
IRS would add a burden at a time when I needed fewer.

I found some happiness taking care of Mary's three
sons, Simeon, Delbert, and Rashad (named for Ahmad).
They stayed at my home on weekends, and we had good
times together, romping in the yard and splashing in the
pool. Uncle Harvey's own undistinguished childhood now
looked sunny and bright to him.

I also spent a lot of time with Mom. My adverse
publicity had weighed heavily on her. Many of her friends
provided little more comfort to her than mine did for me.
During the good times they had seldom mentioned my
great success as a player to her; now they often called to
talk about cocaine. People who had watched me win co-
MVP in Super Bowl XII and never offered Mom a word of
congratulation felt free to tut-tut to their hearts' content.

"I went to the top with my boy," Mom told one
of these people, "and I'll go to the bottom with him, if I
have to."

"You won't have to," I told her. "I'm not a bottom-
type person."

In February 1983 Dwight White called and told me to
be very careful. He'd grown up in Dallas, and never
trusted the city.

Friends told me that at restaurants they often heard my
name mentioned in connection with cocaine—all holier-
than-thou stuff, never tempered with a trace of forgive-

ness. Finally a friend of mine exploded at one of these uninformed experts: "What Harvey mainly did wrong was get caught with the wrong person."

True!

I know I never should have used cocaine. But I was no angel, and with the tremendous pressure I'd been under, I hadn't been strong enough to resist. My crime hadn't been coldblooded or aimed at hurting anybody.

I became a virtual prisoner in my own home. I didn't just imagine people saying negative things when I went out in public—I heard them, and it hurt. I'd been one of the most popular people in Dallas; now I'd become one of the most criticized.

I looked for a place to escape and thought perhaps Mexico might lift my sunken spirits. Mexico had adopted the Cowboys as her own, and south of the border they cheered us as Number One. All our games were broadcast in Spanish back to Mexico, and without question we ranked as that nation's most popular U.S. team.

More important to me at the moment, I'd heard that *my* popularity stood extremely high. A Mexican radio station conducted a poll to determine the country's favorite Cowboy, and I finished first. Too Tall followed in second place. Surprisingly to me, we ranked ahead of our great Mexican kicker, Rafael Septien.

Dallas probably would have voted me least popular.

I decided to take a vacation in Acapulco. Even if I didn't find a warm welcome, I'd get away from chilly Dallas. Shortly before leaving, I received a tempting offer. How would I like to play Mr. Applegate in the upcoming stage production of *Damn Yankees*? The director, Buss Shurr, had seen me in a commercial and thought I'd be ideal for the role. There weren't any other offers, and I'd always wanted to give acting a chance. My only previous experience had been in the movie *Mean Joe Greene and the Pittsburgh Kid*. I said I'd take the script to Mexico and study it there.

I flew to Acapulco with a friend, Bonnie, and we checked into Las Brisas Hotel, which featured a private swimming pool for each room. Bonnie and I strolled over to Pepe Vella's Restaurant, which had come highly recommended, and while I soaked up the warm Mexican sun outside, she went upstairs to make dinner reservations.

"Who's that man downstairs?" Pepe asked Bonnie.

"Harvey Martin."

"The great football player?"

"None other."

"Bring him up! Bring him up!"

Pepe treated me as if I were a visiting head of state, or at least like the head of state's wife, as I'd soon learn. It didn't take long to realize it would be this way all over Acapulco. Adults and little kids rushed up to me; amid their Spanish, I understood only the words *Harvey Martin* and *Dallas Cowboys*. Their warm friendly smiles translated as sincere welcomes to their country and mentally transported me a million miles away from Dallas and ugly talk of cocaine.

Pepe insisted we stay at Villa Vera, and arranged for our move. Villa Vera offered natural clay tennis courts, beautiful sculpture, magnificent restaurants, and a breathtaking view of Acapulco Bay. I knew I'd found a slice of heaven.

"It's where all the movie stars stay," Pepe said.

Maybe some of their talent will rub off on me, I hoped, thinking of *Damn Yankees*.

That night while dining in Pepe's fine restaurant, a poodle ran past my leg, startling me. I looked down, and then up, as Bonnie whispered, "Mrs. Lopez-Portillo is here. Her husband just retired as president of Mexico."

Along with Mrs. Lopez-Portillo came a large entourage, including the former ministers of defense and state.

Mrs. Lopez-Portillo knew of me! She came over and shook my hand, made a fuss, and asked Bonnie and me to have dinner with them. We quickly accepted. She made me promise that if the Cowboys got to the Super Bowl during the next season, I'd send her and her husband tickets to the game.

Mexico did wonders for my flagging spirits. Bonnie and I visited numerous nightclubs and, at Mrs. Lopez-Portillo's insistence, sat at tables normally reserved for her. For a few days I relived the honeymoon years I'd had in Dallas. Wherever I went people patted my back and asked for autographs. Somehow I'd gotten in a time machine and journeyed back to a happier period in my life.

I found time to read the script for *Damn Yankees*, based on the book *The Year the Yankees Lost the Pennant*. The movie had captivated me as a kid. Ray Walston as Mr. Applegate made a lasting impression, and I looked forward, with considerable humility, to playing the part.

Refreshed, I decided that if jobs wouldn't come to me, I'd go to them. I flew from Acapulco to New York City to see if I could line up some network assignments. I needed to put together a resume tape of my past TV appearances, and Ithaca College agreed to do the job in exchange for my speaking to sports broadcasting classes. I'd be a college lecturer, no less!

I loved it. The teachers treated me well, and the kids brimmed with healthy curiosity. One night I went for beer with some college students and had a great time. They wanted to know if Tom Landry ever smiled. I told them I couldn't be sure, but probably not. They asked me my choice for best running back in the NFL. I told them Walter Payton.

In New York City I picked up my tapes at ABC for "Superteams" and also visited CBS and NBC. The only negative note came from a lady at CBS, who felt obliged to say as I was leaving, "Harvey, you be sure to stay out of trouble." This "enlightened" New Yorker evidently felt a black man had to be treated like a child.

I returned to Dallas, grateful I had something besides

getting ready for the coming football season to keep me busy.

If I had any illusions acting would be easy, they were quickly dispelled. Not only did I have to adapt to live stage acting; I had to learn techniques peculiar to theater-in-the-round. The revolving stage at Granny's Dinner Theater (now Star Garden) has been regarded as a challenge by many seasoned actors on national tours. The work proved mentally and physically strenuous, and *Damn Yankees* director Buss Shurr proved almost as tough a taskmaster as Tom Landry. Much of the credit for the play's success belongs to him.

Blonde, beautiful Misty Rowe played Lola, and I believe when we sang "You Gotta Have Heart," we were a true team.

Misty and I went to a Texas Rangers baseball game, sitting in one of the enclosed boxes. Misty enjoyed having rich middle-aged men make fools of themselves over her. Her Marilyn Monroe body and smile turned a lot of heads. She jokingly said chocolate made her sensuous, which prompted a wealthy Texan to send her two cases of Hershey's Chocolate Syrup.

I found Misty sweet, a thrill to be around. During rehearsals we worked from 10 A.M. to 5 P.M., and when the day ended, I was soaked with sweat. That was fine with me. People in the *Damn Yankees* production believed in Harvey Martin, placing them in a minority, and I didn't intend to let them down.

Damn Yankees wasn't my first acting opportunity. Earlier I'd been offered a part in the movie version of Pete Gent's *North Dallas Forty,* which led to the *only* call I've ever received from Cowboys president Tex Schramm.

"I don't agree with the book," he said. "You know, here in the office we don't like the book."

I liked the book. But I didn't want trouble with Tex Schramm, so I bowed out of the movie.

Schramm told the media *North Dallas Forty* was "a

total lie." Gent, he said, had a "sick approach to life." What Gent mainly could do was write effectively about the dehumanizing business aspects of professional football.

The Cowboys' organization can be counted on not to like any work that detracts from their America's Team image, and the dislike may not be entirely passive. I know the producers intended to film *North Dallas Forty* in Dallas, but they got moved out. They tried Houston, but things didn't work out there either. So the movie got shot in Los Angeles.

Earlier the Cowboys objected to the X-rated movie *Debbie Does Dallas*. I'll let authors Mark Nelson and Miller Bonner tell the story:

> Ol' Debbie did New York and Los Angeles and a lot of points in between, but she ran into trouble when she tried to do Big D. The 90-minute film about a woman hoping to try out for the Dallas Cowboys Cheerleaders and finding all sorts of erotic adventures was shown twice in Dallas in February 1979.
>
> The Cowboys called the vice squad.
>
> The Dallas Corporates filed suit claiming that "Debbie Does Dallas" was obscene and specifically objected to the similarity between the uniforms worn by Debbie and her mates and the real Dallas Cowboys Cheerleaders uniforms.

The Cowboys won the lawsuit. All references to the uniforms and the Dallas cheerleaders had to be deleted from the film.

Some former Dallas Cowboy cheerleaders took the name Dallas Cowgirls to model and appear at trade shows. The Cowboys took the Cowgirls to court. They forced a name change to the Dallas Girls, and made the ex-cheerleaders include a disclaimer in all promotional and advertising material.

Jeanie Cavett, one of the ex-cheerleaders, said, "It's just like an ex-football player using his name to start his

own business. No one can take away the fact that we were once cheerleaders for the Cowboys. And because of that, people want to meet us. We're not doing anything wrong. Suzanne Mitchell [director of the cheerleaders] knew we were in business for about two years and she didn't say a thing. But when she turned down a TV commercial, the company called us and we did the commercial. That was it. The next thing I know it's in the newspaper that the Cowboys were mad, and I got served legal papers the same day. They never said anything to me. But they would call clients and try to scare them off. It certainly doesn't help business."

The Cowboys always talk about the wholesome image the cheerleaders provide, though one of their former members saw it differently.

We were selling sex. They would pull our shorts up higher on our legs so our butts would show. We were required to wear push-up bras. The whole thing revolved around butts and cleavage. For them to say we were good little virgin girls is ludicrous.

During one game, one of the girls was doing a cheer and one of her breasts popped right out of her uniform. The crowd loved it. That's what we were there for.

With the exception of a negative review in the *Dallas Morning News* (the *Times Herald* was very favorable), most people thought I did a first-rate job as Mr. Applegate. A number of individuals quite frankly admitted they had bought tickets to see me mess up. They wanted to see the football player stumble over his feet and his lines. "I came to laugh at you," I heard often, "but I left the theater impressed."

During the run of *Damn Yankees,* the specter of cocaine once again reared its head. To understand what happened, you need to know that a big bust of Brazilians took place around the time of the trial of Snow White and Danny Stone.

I was a friend of Walder Martins, a black Brazilian soccer player, formerly with the Dallas Tornadoes. Walder was from Sao Paolo and knew Pele. He'd worked for me three years and managed Recipe's. Later he took up with a tough crowd, started selling cocaine, and became associated with The Crazy Chicken, where he dealt drugs. Despite these considerable negatives, I liked the man personally and didn't break off my friendship with him. I used poor judgment, but nothing more was involved.

"What are you doing with these guys?" I often asked Walder. I hoped he'd find a different line of work.

And as a matter of fact, he completely divorced himself from the cocaine business before the bust of the other Brazilians took place. When that occurred, the FBI called me at the practice field and said they wanted to talk to me. Then they called again and said we didn't have to talk.

After the arrest of the Brazilians I told Walder he and I shouldn't be seen together anymore. It turned out to be an intelligent decision because the arrested Brazilians soon named Walder as the kingpin of the operation, a completely untrue allegation that simply served their purposes: setting the blame off on someone else.

Coach Landry sensed another impending eruption of scandal and tried to stop it. This led to my fourth and last meeting (actually a series of meetings on the same subject) with him. Landry called while I was performing a Sunday matinee of *Damn Yankees*. I got back to him later in the afternoon. "I want you to talk to Larry Wansley," he said. "Later I'd like to talk to you."

The Cowboys had hired Wansley, a former FBI agent, to keep an eye on the activities of players—to spy on them. I met with Wansley at the Cowboy offices.

"There's a guy downtown," Wansley said, "an assistant United States attorney, who feels he has enough on a lot of the players to send them to jail."

"I don't know what you're talking about," I said.

"We need you guys to cooperate."

"You guys?"

"This U.S. attorney wants to prosecute. He means business. I've seen the evidence, and it's powerful."

"What evidence?"

"I can't tell you that."

Wansley didn't bother to tell me that the attorney had *no* evidence against me. I did learn of taps on The Crazy Chicken telephones, photographs taken of Cowboys going in and out of The Crazy Chicken, and photographs of Cowboys making drug transactions. None of these incriminated me in any way. My "crime" was knowing Walder. It turned out the Brazilians had been *making cocaine* in Dallas.

In exchange for a lesser sentence, the South Americans offered to give the FBI the names of Dallas Cowboys they claimed were involved with them. There were eight in all, including Ron Springs, Larry Bethea, Tony Dorsett, and Tony Hill. I was given the names of four other Cowboys against whom the government said it had insufficient evidence to prosecute, so their names won't be mentioned here.

As much as anyone, I knew the Cowboy roster included no altar boys, and never had—except maybe Roger Staubach.

Walder called me at my home and I taped the conversation. He said the U.S. attorney wanted his name in the newspapers and figured an excellent way to accomplish that would be to indict some big-name football players. Walder admitted in this conversation that I'd had no knowledge of the Dallas cocaine lab and emphasized that he'd quit selling the drug before the feds busted the Brazilians.

I met with Coach Landry.

He said, "I feel if we show that we as an organization are trying to curtail these wild activities, the government will ease up. You're a leader, Harvey. I'd like you to go to

Hazelden and come back and report to the team. Bring back as much literature as you can. Talk to the players about what you learn."

Hazelden is a drug and alcohol rehabilitation facility just outside Minneapolis.

"We sent him there to evaluate the program for us," Landry told the press, "not to dry out. I don't feel he's involved with drugs right now."

I knew what Landry meant by "wild activities." Some younger players had become obvious embarrassments to the Cowboys, with obnoxious, blatant displays of public drunkenness. And the public was only one newspaper story away from finding out.

Up to that time I believe Landry wrapped himself up in football so much that he didn't know what went on off the field. To his credit, when he learned, he moved with all possible speed to clean things up.

I didn't want to go to Hazelden, but I never said no to Coach Landry. I'd do almost anything the man asked me. I'm glad I made the trip, but the later publicity from it caused me terrific anguish.

Drug center and *Harvey Martin* became indelibly linked in the public's mind. Fans, the media, and even teammates quickly expressed skepticism of my motives. Still, at Hazelden, I *saw* what I didn't want to become. There were patients whose lives had been totally shattered by drugs.

I flew to Minnesota with Larry Wansley, who had been a cop, and took the program. At Hazelden they explain why you have a problem, get you clean, and show you how to stay that way. The nation could use hundreds of low-cost Hazeldens.

I'd agreed to go knowing I had nothing to hide. Although I'd been under terrific pressure, I wasn't addicted to any drugs. Nevertheless the stay at Hazelden brought a wave of unwanted headlines. The first to appear, in the

May 28, 1983, *Dallas Morning News* read, "COWBOYS'
MARTIN IN REHAB CENTER."

The public nodded its collective head and said, Uh
huh.

Tom Landry explained, but nobody listened: "About
ten days to two weeks ago, I had Harvey come in. What I
wanted to do was get one of our leaders to go to the
rehabilitation clinic and evaluate it for us, and when he
came back, give a positive witness to what took place to
any player who wants to go there."

An unnamed teammate questioned the explanation:
"Now, why would Harvey put himself through this if he
didn't have a problem? He's got nothing to gain by doing
this for the Cowboys unless he needs the help. I'm just
glad they didn't ask me, because there's no way I would
do it."

That teammate may have been thinking more clearly
than I was.

Randy Galloway of the *Dallas Morning News* wrote
what I consider one of the fairer stories:

Tom Landry has been around long enough to know better,
but he says it was a story he never expected the newspapers to
cover. . . .

Unfortunately, Tom fumbled that one.

When he saw the story in print Saturday morning, he knew
that confusion would follow, he knew that people would attempt
to make something out of what he insists is nothing. And he also
had to know that Martin's name would be dragged through the
rumor mud. Again. It's just been that kind of year for Harvey.

However, when it comes down to a game of who-do-you-
believe, Tom Landry can score at will against anyone. You read
the newspaper stories Saturday on Martin being in Minnesota,
and the explanation seemed perfectly ridiculous. Even to other
Cowboy players, as their quotes indicated. But would Tom
Landry lie to us?

Not in 23 years. At least no falsehood has been duly recorded in that span, which is the nicest thing you can say about someone who has spent almost a lifetime under close public scrutiny. . . .

But, as Galloway pointed out, the visit to Hazelden "did Harvey Martin no good once the media became aware of it." Galloway asked why I was the one chosen.

"Because he's been through so much lately," Landry answered, "because he's suffered, and because he's come out of it with a really great attitude, is the very reason I asked him to go. What better spokesman could there be to go there and actually participate in something like this?"

Mom, bless her heart, decided she couldn't take anymore and spoke out in the *Dallas Morning News*. "If I was Harvey," she said, "I would have told Tom Landry no. I'm telling you I would have told Harvey not to volunteer to go. But I'm not Harvey. If I wasn't his mother and knew he wasn't on drugs, I would believe it."

That was just the point. I myself might have believed another player had a drug problem if the excuse offered for him had been the one the Cowboys offered for me, no matter how true.

"I'm sorry his visit became public," said Landry. "I can see where there would be confusion on this, but it's just not what some people are going to think."

Mom, given the opportunity, made sure she got her say. "I wish Harvey had more of me than just my legs and looks. He doesn't have my mind. I'm very bitter. I'd let no one do to me what Harvey has had done to him. Harvey is a good, decent person and doesn't deserve this. If he learned how to hate, I would be happy for him. Harvey forgives if you do him wrong."

Tell 'em, Mom: "Give Harvey a break. They don't have anything on my son but everybody wants to crucify him. He can't make any money in Dallas. He can't even get an autograph-signing job. Who wants him signing autographs when they think he's in a rehabilitation center?

I am so sick and tired of this. I wish Harvey would quit playing football so people could find another black to pick on. If this happened to a white boy, it wouldn't even be in the papers."

Indeed. When Randy White, who rightly has never been accused of using drugs, later paid a visit to Hazelden, *no one* suggested he'd gone for treatment. Though Randy didn't check into the clinic, and other circumstances were dissimilar, he did go to gather information, as I had.

I told only one Cowboy, Don Smerek, that I'd be going to Hazelden. "I'll prove I'm clean," I said to Smerek. The urine tests I took and passed upon arrival proved my point—and also what Coach Landry later told the press.

There was a big-name politician receiving treatment at Hazelden when I arrived. As if his drug problems weren't enough, he kept receiving calls from a reporter who wanted to make the story public. It seemed unfair to me, at least the timing. Shedding a drug problem poses a monumental enough task without having to worry about the press.

I soon identified with this politician. *Dallas Morning News* reporter Gary Myers called Hazelden seeking information about me. Although I couldn't be sure, I figured Don Smerek had told Myers, which didn't make me happy with my teammate.

Myers soon printed a story containing a quote from my friend Butch Johnson, one of the few Cowboys who didn't think I was either a fool or in need of treatment. "Harvey has been through a lot," Butch said. "He's been through the spectrum of the profession from Super Bowl Most Valuable Player to bankruptcy. He would understand what's going on. That's why I think they chose him."

Some Cowboy players said they weren't interested in hearing me lecture on drugs but, as Landry pointed out, that wasn't the point. "It is not the intent for Harvey to come back and start confronting the players. That is not going to happen. That's not why he made the visit. But down the way, if we come across another Thomas Henderson, then there's nothing the matter with me saying, 'Harvey, why don't you tell him what you know?' "

As soon as Myers called, I felt I'd made a mistake going to Hazelden. Drug treatment and Harvey Martin would forever be linked in the public's mind, no matter what Coach Landry said, no matter that I'd passed the drug test. The Cowboys should have found somebody else to go to Hazelden, I thought angrily.

I would have packed my bags and left right then, but Coach Landry telephoned me. "You're doing this for the team," he emphasized.

Landry knew if he talked about the team, the Cowboys, whom I loved, I'd do anything he asked.

Ernie Stautner adopted the same tack: "I'm glad you're doing this for the team," he said when I called him to express reservations about staying.

But, as is obvious, it came out differently in the Dallas media. The press in Dallas became so overeager to cover the story that the Cowboys deemed it advisable to purchase two different plane tickets for my flight from Minneapolis to Dallas. The team didn't want me deluged by a mob of reporters when I returned home.

The press met one plane; I slipped into Dallas on another. I'd avoided one unpleasant scene, but up ahead lay others that would be much worse.

Shortly after returning from Hazelden, I went to Coach Landry. "I'm back," I said. "I feel good."

"The press is here," Landry said. "They're going to ask some questions. I want you to tell the truth. Tell them why you went to Hazelden. Then I'll talk to them and back you up."

The press bared its teeth like wolves toward me, the sacrificial lamb. I told them I went to Hazelden so I could help the team, report back to teammates what I'd learned, and that the trip had helped me, too, because it opened my eyes to the dangers of drugs. Coach Landry backed me up.

The situation deteriorated. The press conference didn't convince anybody of the true reason for my trip to Hazelden. I couldn't remember Dallas ever doubting Coach Landry's word before, but this time it did.

For my own part, I hadn't known at first how deep the Brazilian/Crazy Chicken/Cowboys connection really went. Younger teammates had walked into The Crazy Chicken as routinely as if strolling into a fast-food joint to order a hamburger, unknowingly posing for hidden cameras as they made cocaine purchases.

A woman reporter for the *Dallas Morning News* called me and said she planned a story indicating that Tony

Dorsett and I had admitted to the FBI that we used cocaine. I had used cocaine—and regretted it—but I hadn't been addicted, hadn't admitted it, and had never talked to the FBI. Besides, none of this was any of the paper's business.

I told the reporter the story wasn't true and asked her not to run it. My lawyer also told her, but of course the story ran anyway.

I thought of suing but decided such action would only result in more unfavorable publicity. I came to dread reading the paper each day. Dallas was my hometown, and I felt an especial disgrace. I also felt terrible for Tony Dorsett, who suffered from a whisper campaign and, like me, in more tangible ways. He lost many endorsements as employers turned away from him *en masse*.

Damned if I did, damned if I didn't, I determined not to let the negative publicity drive me into isolation and seclusion. In the evenings I'd go to the Memphis Restaurant and Bar and just stand around, making myself visible and hoping people realized I had nothing to hide.

But nothing helped. "You might as well be Henry Lee Lucas," a friend told me, comparing the perception the public had of me to that of the confessed serial killer.

The roof got blown off when Tony Hill and I were subpoenaed to testify at the Brazilians' trial.

The public anticipated that Tony and I would say we had bought drugs. Actually, we'd been subpoenaed to testify that we hadn't. The defendant whose lawyer subpoenaed us thought it would count in his favor for us to testify truthfully that we'd bought no drugs from him. It turned out our testimony wasn't needed, but the subpoena left us associated in the public mind with courts and cocaine.

The New York Times broke the story about five Cowboys—naming me but not the four others—allegedly involved in cocaine. That made the story national. I didn't care about the national element. It was Dallas, my hometown, where I had to live, that I cared about. And Dallas's attitude wasn't as forgiving as New York's.

Until then I'd always stayed in top-notch physical condition in anticipation of training camp, but that year I didn't. After Hazelden I slacked off.

I *liked* to work out, but the repeated cocaine allegations got to me. I couldn't break free of the worry, anxiety, and depression to get myself up to the physical level needed to compete in the NFL.

Walder Martins pleaded guilty to an old charge of selling cocaine and was not put on trial. But other of the Brazilians were brought into court. The news stories made me feel *I* stood accused in the dock.

One of the defendants, testifying in his own behalf, was asked if I knew cocaine was being manufactured in Dallas. "No," he said, "Harvey knew nothing."

I reported to Thousand Oaks in poor shape. To make matters worse, most of my teammates studiously avoided me—the Drew Pearson syndrome. Billy Joe DuPree and Benny Barnes were the exceptions. They helped a great deal, merely by talking to me, by being seen with me.

Nineteen eighty-three would be the last in football for Drew, Billy Joe, Benny, and myself. Billy Joe retired, and Drew sustained injuries in an automobile accident.

The player I felt worst about was Benny Barnes. He'd wanted to retire earlier; he hadn't even wanted to come to camp. But management had pleaded with this most popular (among his teammates) of Cowboys to come back for one more year "for the good of the team." Management assured Benny he had a secure position on the roster. So he went through the terrible rigors of an entire training camp—and then they cut him. This action saddened all of us and reemphasized the shabby treatment a veteran player too often gets. Instead of the dignified retirement Benny wanted, he simply got cut from the team, discarded like an old pair of shoes.

Very early in training camp I hurt my shoulder and couldn't practice. Even combing my hair became impossible. But just as big a problem came from the anxiety caused by all the drug stories. Along with my injured shoulder, each day the Cowboys' doctor checked my blood pressure. Not being able to practice concerned me, but, foolishly perhaps, I thought my years as All-Pro, being voted the NFL's Most Valuable Defensive Player, winning the Super Bowl co-MVP award, and my record in three Super Bowls would protect my job.

Two things need to be understood about my shoulder injury: (1) It is an unwritten rule that regulars do not play in preseason games if they are injured; and (2) my shoulder would have healed if given more rest.

However, I was put into an exhibition game against the Miami Dolphins and aggravated the injury. I came off the field in terrific pain. Cowboy doctor Mervin Knight shot my right arm with pain-killer and said I could go back in and play. On just the second down after my reappearance, I hurt the shoulder badly. Shocks of pain assailed me, nearly blinded me, even through the pain-killer. Even *today* my arm still hurts.

Did the Cowboys play me when I was injured because they were angry about the national attention brought about by the drug trials? Did they deliberately set out to hurt me? I hope not. But I had told Dr. Knight I didn't think I should play in the Miami exhibition and I had protested again when he shot me full of pain-killer and said I could go back in.

The injury forced me to make a major change in my style of playing football. I had to switch from a right-hand-down stance to a left-hand-down stance because I couldn't get my right hand all the way to the ground. In one sense I had to start learning football all over again. A hell of a note for a ten-year veteran! I didn't have a good opening season game against the Redskins, but how could I? I'd started behind in training camp and then missed much of practice. What I wanted to do, what I thought I'd earned, was the right to play my way into shape. I'd been a key member of the Cowboys for a decade, leading the team in sacks *every year,* and I deserved that much consideration.

But the press soon screamed for my job. Why is Harvey Martin still starting? sportswriters wanted to know. Reporter Jim Dent made a crack about my leaving my playing on the stage, a reference to my altogether worthwhile appearance in *Damn Yankees.* Maybe he would have talked about "dumb jocks" if he'd known I'd loaded Dr. Pepper trucks.

I appreciated Landry letting me *start* every game, but was humiliated at being taken out early to be replaced by either Larry Bethea or Jim Jeffcoat. Bethea would never approach my ability as a player; and Jeffcoat, although tough and talented, was too young and inexperienced. The press mercilessly criticized my performance, which many people blamed on drugs. In reality the causes were an injury, personal worries, and being out of condition.

The Cowboys won their first seven games of the regular season. "We're winning!" Tony Hill would bubble, and wonder why I looked morose.

Although I felt happiness for my teammates, I didn't feel myself part of it. Worst of all was the humiliation. I'd start the games and then get benched. I didn't get put in even on pass-rushing downs, my specialty, at which I had no peer. When I wasn't sitting all alone at the end of the bench, feeling humiliated, I was standing behind Ernie Stautner, begging him to put me in. It embarrassed both of us. Football wasn't fun for me anymore.

You're not a quitter, Harvey, I told myself and literally

willed myself to return to what I'd been. I worked ardu-
ously with Cowboy conditioning coach Bob Ward to
strengthen my shoulder. I lifted weights and did sit-ups,
exerted myself like a Trojan. Ward was wonderful. He
never gave up on me, and with his help I got back into top-
flight condition. Ward began wondering out loud why I
kept getting pulled out of games.

In the fifth from last game of the regular season I
played well against Kansas City, but once again I was
pulled out early. We won 41–21. The next week, a 35–17
victory over St. Louis, I kept waiting to be yanked. I'd
look over my shoulder, expecting to see Jeffcoat or Bethea, but they never came. *Well*, I thought, *it's playoff
time. A time for the stars!*

In the last few games of the season I became my old
self. I'd come back with one arm, great pride, and a
weight coach. The newspapers started trumpeting, "Harvey is back!"

Before I began playing games start to finish, Coach
Landry had a talk with me. "I want you to take a drug
test," he said.

"For what?"

"For drugs."

"Coach, this is ridiculous."

I broke down and cried in front of Landry. "You don't
let me play anymore," I said. "You have me competing
against Larry Bethea, who never bought a breakfast for
the Cowboys, and a rookie, Jeffcoat, who'll be good
someday, but isn't ready yet."

"Well," Landry said, "you're getting in more." He
hesitated. "Now."

"I want to think about that test," I said.

I contacted Larry Wansley and asked if he had any
idea what was going on. "I think it's got to do with
Memphis," he said, referring to the restaurant I'd fre-
quented. Cowboy management had barred all the Cow-

boys from going there, a ban I honored. "I think," Wansley added, "people are selling drugs there."

So that was it. I knew Cowboy security director Larry Wansley, a former FBI agent, had seen me in Memphis. He'd spent a good deal of his time shadowing me and other Cowboys. Earlier Wansley had turned the Cowboys' training camp at Thousand Oaks into what sportswriters dubbed "Fort Landry." He set up checkpoints, barricades, and round-the-clock security patrols. Regardless, plenty of players still sneaked out.

"It has to be done," Landry told me. So I took the drug test and again came up clean. Fifteen other Cowboys were told to take the drug tests after I passed mine. I vowed to myself that I'd never take another one—this made twice that I'd been asked to trailblaze. *Three strikes and you're out,* I thought.

I played excellent football the last few games of the regular season and into the playoffs. But I remained, uncharacteristically, a loner, staying away from other players.

One day Ernie Stautner found me sitting alone in a meeting room. He came up and put his hand on my knee. "You know, Harvey," he said, "my hands were tied when we put you through all this; but I want you to know I'm proud of you. You pulled out of it good."

I appreciated the compliment. But I wondered how they could take back all the suffering.

We lost to the Rams 24–17 in the playoffs, our problem being too many holes in the offensive line. The offensive line just didn't have what it took. They got called for too many holding penalties. They simply lacked the needed competitive fire. They weren't fierce enough. They were just as big as anybody else, just as talented, but they didn't click *as a team,* the way the glory year Cowboys had.

I don't know why I acted as I did after the playoff loss

to the Rams. Maybe my subconscious saw the future. I told Buck Buchanan, Cowboy equipment manager, to give me my jersey. I've wondered since if Buck also saw the future. "You know, Harvey," he said, "you ended up real good for yourself."

I had "ended up real good." After being reinjured in the Miami game, a Cowboy doctor had tested my arm and it had *no* strength whatever. A useless appendage. Through determination and Bob Ward's help, I had got it back to where I could play up to my own high standards. I intended to keep it that way. I immediately began working out in the off-season, under Bob Ward's tutelage. I was the only player on the team doing this arduous conditioning so early, and I brought myself to a state of superior condition that I intended to maintain right up to training camp and into the season.

I accepted a position during the off-season as sales manager for PCB Electronics, a minority-owned business that sold printed circuit boards. I was once again back in the mainstream, and it felt good.

I reported to veterans camp as frisky as I'd once been at East Texas State. As the Dean, I had to do everything first, and I did it with relish—running, jumping, yelling, feeling great.

After grueling workout sessions, I enjoyed driving to the practice field where my cousin Roy Martin trained. One of the fastest sprinters in the country, today he is one of the favorites to capture gold in the 1988 Olympics. I also surrounded myself with Mary's children, having them stay with me on weekends, swimming and playing catch with them and basking in their youthful exuberance. I'd be good this coming year, I knew. I'd really open some eyes. My body burst with strength and good health.

It took only an instant to deflate me and bring back all the old nightmares.

One day after a strenuous workout, when I was exhausted and wanting only to relax, Larry Wansley walked up to me. He had a urine specimen bottle in his hand. "We need to take a sample," he said.

I thought of all the years I'd given 100 percent to the Cowboys, of taking Art Shell's deliberately hurting me, of a thousand bone-jarring hits I'd taken "for the team," of going to Hazelden and getting burned for it, of a shot of pain-killer that crippled, of so much more, and I exploded.

"Fuck you!" I screamed at Larry Wansley.

"We need it," he said softly.

"I retire!" I yelled at him.

The Cowboys thought I was bullshitting, and they couldn't have been more wrong. How much humiliation did they expect me to take? One time as I signed autographs for young children, a newspaper reporter started asking me about drugs. Now here came Wansley, people watching, and he wanted me to piss into a bottle.

I called the NFLPA (the players union) and talked with Gene Upshaw, the director and former great of the Oakland Raiders. Old Highway 63, so named for his uniform number, Upshaw worked as tenaciously in the interests of players as he had demolishing defenses as an All-Pro offensive guard. "How can they do this to me?" I asked Upshaw.

"They can't," Upshaw laughed. "Well, we've got something on the Cowboys now," he said. "They always bragged we wouldn't, but I thought we would, and I guess I win."

The Cowboys had no right to ask me to take a drug test. I'd done it in the past "for the team," but enough was enough. Previously, I thought sadly, the Cowboys' Number One interest had been how you performed on the field—whether you won—not what happened in the privacy of your home. They once had been like the Raiders, a band of misfits (although the Cowboys' management certainly cultivated a different image) whose job was to win football games.

I went into seclusion in my home. I didn't want to see

anyone. I didn't want this whole nightmare to start again. But I did venture out once to make a point—a major point, I thought. I visited a doctor, took and *passed* a drug test on my own, and later released the results to Bob St. John of the *Dallas Morning News*. I decided that there was a difference between taking a drug test of my own volition and being forced into it by Larry Wansley.

I continued to work out by myself at home, but the "I retire!" I'd yelled at Wansley seemed more appealing by the day. No matter what I did, how I comported myself, I could see I'd be a target as long as I remained a Dallas Cowboy. I thought I'd literally have to flee from the harsh spotlight to find peace of mind.

Coach Landry kept calling and leaving messages for me to get in touch with him, but I didn't return his calls. Instead I pondered my future and made tentative checks with people I trusted.

"I think I'm really going to quit," I told my Mom.

"Son, you do what you think is best."

I called Dwight White. "Retire," said Mad Dog. "You're overdue, anyway." Dwight reminded me what happened to Rayfield, Cornell, and Bob Hayes. A black player toward the end of his career didn't have a chance in Dallas, he said.

I talked to Rayfield. "Quit, man," he advised. "It's driving you crazy. Nothing is worth this." Rayfield had earlier advised me *not* to retire. That time I guess he felt I needed to prove something; this time I had nothing left to prove.

A sense of sad, subdued finality descended on me.

I got together with Mom. She sensibly put pencil to paper and figured out how much money I had. It was enough. I didn't need to go through any more physical punishment only to be tortured by off-field innuendoes. The $300,000 I would have received for 1984 was tempting, but no amount of money would compensate for

another year of having my name raked through the muck
and seeing my mother suffer.

I thought it a good time to go away. I'd been the old
Harvey those last few games of the 1983 season, full of life
and terrorizing quarterbacks, and I wanted fans to remember me that way. That would be good: Mention Harvey
Martin's name, and people would think of an all-out rush,
a fear-stricken quarterback, a drive-ending sack.

I made arrangements to go to Acapulco. Mexico would
be a warm haven for me when the inevitable stories
misstating the reasons for my retirement appeared. As
I've said, football just wasn't any fun anymore; the emphasis had changed from winning to ferreting out drug
usage. It made me feel terrible when I saw kids on dope—
girls selling their bodies for drugs, young boys shattering
their lives before life really began. Nor did I want my
name linked with any of the younger players who'd
pranced right into The Crazy Chicken, not a sensible
thought in their heads, parading like fools for FBI cameras. I figured I'd already taken much of *their* heat.

I drove to the Cowboy offices with Mitchell Greenstein, the friend I was going to Acapulco with, and waited
for Coach Landry . . . and waited. I wanted him to know
first. I respected him more than any other man. Finally I
called Coach Landry at his home.

"I'm retiring," I said.

"Take a couple of weeks to think about it, Harvey.
Don't do it now."

My state of mind was such that momentarily I couldn't
even trust Coach Landry. *If I give him two weeks,* I
thought, *he might trade me to Buffalo in the interim.*

"No," I said firmly. "I'm retiring now."

I didn't add "while I've still got a trace of dignity left."

"Harvey," Landry said, "you need to hold a press
conference. A player of your magnitude needs to go out
the right way."

"I've got a flight to Acapulco tomorrow," I said. "It will have to be first thing in the morning.

So I met the press the next morning, May 31, 1984, at the Twin Sixties Motel, near the Cowboy offices. I couldn't keep myself from being all choked up, remembering the good times—no, the *great* times. This must be what people experience during a particularly heartbreaking divorce, I thought.

Mom came. And Ernie Stautner. And Coach Landry, bless him, stood right by my side.

Tex Schramm and Gil Brandt made themselves look bad by not bothering to make an appearance for a player who, according to *Times Herald* columnist Skip Bayless, had in 1977 "possibly the greatest season ever by a defensive end. Too Mean: 23 sacks, 85 tackles, Super MVP."

I'd helped give the Cowboys three Super Bowls and a world championship. But what did I expect? Rayfield hadn't received any better, and I wasn't any better than Rayfield.

Skip Bayless described the scene:

Martin stands tall before a group that has come more to bury than praise him. This is not the loving tribute to retiring "B. J." DuPree. This is Martin, briefly saying all the right things and rushing out, ushered by his mother, to "catch a plane." This is absent Tex Schramm and Gil Brandt, who almost always attend these affairs, probably thankful to be rid of Harvey's headlines. This is Wansley, perhaps sweating the possibility that Martin will say too much, about himself and other Cowboys. . . .

Many Cowboys said they weren't happy with the way Martin was treated. He's basically a good guy—maybe too good.

"He gave us tremendous leadership," said defensive back Dennis Thurman, "and was one of our main guys for a lot of years."

"He went from a third-round draft choice to a starter

to the Pro Bowl to All-Pro to Most Valuable Player in the Super Bowl," said Billy Joe DuPree. "He led our team in sacks ten of eleven years. But it's sad about the experiences he had in his personal and social life. I think, though, that when all is said and done, he will be remembered as a great player and a pretty sensible guy."

Ernie Stautner attended the retirement press conference. "We're certainly going to miss Harvey," he said. "He's been a great player for us for many years and it's very difficult to replace a player of his caliber. I was surprised. I didn't think he was going to retire this year. I talked to Bob Ward recently, and he indicated Harvey was working hard and his shoulder was improving. I would have liked to see Harvey come back and play again. I know he could have reverted to the Harvey of old with a great degree of motivation."

Stautner added, "Harvey could be the greatest player in the world when he wanted to be."

The greatest player in the world? This was some kind of high praise coming from a Hall of Famer. Stautner's "wanted to be" was just part of our more-than-a-decade argument about whether I always gave my best. I did, and I wish I could have convinced Ernie.

I told the press my reasons for quitting, although I didn't specifically mention Larry Wansley and his urine bottle. I could tell they didn't believe me. A "highly placed" Cowboy official had leaked to the reporters that I'd been faced with an ultimatum: Return to Hazelden or retire. In reality, said the "highly placed" official, the Cowboys wanted me to retire.

Why did this man have to plant malicious doubt? Did he, as Skip Bayless said, want "Dallas fans to jump to a conclusion?" Or did he fear what I might have to say about America's Team—to which I gave much more loyalty than I received—and decide to smear me before I even talked? And why did most of the reporters choose to believe a source they wouldn't even name instead of Tom

Landry, who "can score at will against anyone" when it comes to telling the truth?

Tom Landry spoke words at the press conference that I'll treasure forever:

We're obviously going to miss Harvey. As we look back at his career, he has given us so much. There are so many highlights. He was very instrumental in the great teams we had.

I told him he shouldn't retire, that he should continue to play. But I respect his judgment. You have to do that when you've been associated with a player as long as I have been with Harvey.

Of course, I tried to talk Harvey out of retiring. We didn't want him to go.

EPILOGUE

Tom Landry's words provided warmth for a lifetime, but they were pushed out of mind, however briefly, the instant the press conference ended.

"Isn't it true," one reporter asked, "that you were faced with an ultimatum to leave?"

The question hurt tremendously. It wasn't true, but what difference would that make in how it got reported?

About the Cowboys' wanting me to leave, the exact opposite held true. Larry Bethea had gone to the USFL, and the Cowboys had only Jim Jeffcoat remaining at my position, a player still too young and inexperienced. *Fact:* Landry wanted me to stay. *Fact:* Landry asked me to stay. *Fact:* I was in the best condition of my career.

On the flight to Acapulco, my spirits sank to rock bottom. Coach Landry, perhaps the most credible man in Texas, had told the media, "We didn't want Harvey to leave," and that still hadn't helped.

A husband and wife stopped at my seat on the plane. The man had heard about my retirement. "We're going to miss you," he said.

I stared straight ahead, paying him no attention. Is that what football had made of me? I couldn't remember ever not smiling at a well-wisher or having something friendly to say. My depression overwhelmed me; I feared I was about to cry again. I knew I'd left something I loved.

Later in Acapulco I saw the couple I'd snubbed on the airplane and apologized to them.

Pepe met us at the airport in his limousine, and that evening we dined on a cruise liner docked in Acapulco Bay. Once again I received the royal treatment in Mexico, and almost immediately began feeling better. I'd brought a large number of gifts with me—Cowboy T-shirts, Cowboy posters, and other items—and passed them out at every opportunity. I don't know if you can feel blood pressure dropping, but I *thought* I could. I went to bed early at Villa Vera, totally exhausted but somehow much more relaxed. I could almost feel the problems of the past few years lifting their burdensome weight from my shoulders.

"You're on TV! You're on TV!" shouted Mitchell Greenstein, shaking me awake. I blinked at the television. A Mexican channel carried moment after moment from my career, an entire show of Harvey Martin highlights. I stretched out on the bed and enjoyed watching myself once again pound Jim Hart into the turf. I found myself thinking of other times I wished they'd show—like when I slapped the head of offensive guard Conrad Dobler, reputedly the toughest of the tough, and all Dobler managed was a whimper: "Why did you do that, Harvey?"

"I'm glad you came home to us," Pepe said every time I saw him.

Somehow Mexico did feel like home. I called Mom in Dallas and she told me about the articles appearing in the papers. I thought many of them unfair, but newspapers run what they want. The media even made disparaging remarks about PCB Electronics. The business showed a nice profit but, I felt because a black owned it, the reader was urged to infer that the company operated on subsidies and welfare.

One reporter hinted that my job with PCB represented a ploy for negotiating a higher contract. (Why would I concoct such a preposterous game plan if the Cowboys wanted me gone?) I could have reemphasized until I was hoarse that playing football had turned sour for me, but the message would never break through. Reporters didn't believe Too Tall when he said he wanted to try boxing; they hinted he threatened to enter the ring to squeeze more money from the gridiron. They didn't believe his motives then, nor mine now.

It gave me satisfaction that I'd taken that final drug urine test but, although the results appeared in an article written by Bob St. John, not many minds changed. I refused to care. I'd initiated the test to assure Mom, to show her she didn't have a son who ran from a specimen bottle.

Gradually I started to put my life back together. I achieved a degree of success, I think, because I didn't have so much to worry about. It worked out the opposite of what might have been predicted. Instead of getting out of business to concentrate on football, I left football to concentrate on business.

With funds I'd saved, I started Chase Management Development Company, making myself chairman of the board. Among several successes, I placed a profitable division of the giant Wal-Mart Corporation in my hometown section of South Oak Cliff, an area of the Metroplex other developers ignored in their tooth-and-nail fights over high-dollar real estate ventures in more affluent sections.

With ugly headlines a thing of the past, I once again became active in charity work: Special Olympics, Muscular Dystrophy Association, The Family Place, Wednesday's Child, American Heart Association, Children's Medical Center, and the Parkland Hospital Blood Bank.

The Family Place has a special place in my heart. This is a home for abused and battered wives whose address is kept even from the police. It's important that no male knows its location.

Another activity especially close to my heart is Wednesday's Child, which finds homes for orphans nobody wants.

I stayed involved in football in 1984, doing color commentary of NFL games for NBC. Two years later I had a major role in the movie *No Safe Haven,* and again there were suggestions that I try to succeed full-time as an actor.

At Super Bowl XX, played between the Bears and Patriots in New Orleans, I was honored along with all the other former Super Bowl MVPs in a ceremony before the game. It thrilled me to be on the same field with Bart Starr, leader of Vince Lombardi's legendary Green Bay Packers; Joe Namath, who promised the Jets would defeat the heavily favored Colts in Super Bowl III, and then went out and did it; and Jim Plunkett, a tough Native American whose blind parents, I knew, were rightly proud of their son.

Unfortunately, I thought, John Riggins had also gotten himself a Super Bowl MVP award. His behavior in New Orleans didn't surprise me. He had to be pulled out of a bar to attend a pre-Super Bowl Boy Scout banquet and spent his time during the game drinking large amounts of beer and annoying me. He kept calling me "Haaaarrrrrv," chugging beer, and talking loudly. I'd brought Mom to the Super Bowl, and she sensed what I was about to do.

"He's got no class, Harvey," she said. "Don't hurt him. Don't lower yourself to his level."

Mom was right. I wouldn't let Riggins, a Redskin, put a blemish on a weekend filled with such warm nostalgia. Watching Richard Dent, who was named MVP of the game, I'd even caught myself thinking how similar our games were. *Go after them, Richard,* I thought. I knew how he must feel on *his* biggest day. The Bears routed the Patriots almost the same way we had crushed the Orange of Denver, and on the same field.

In 1986 I participated in a fun production called Wrestlemania II, the most spectacular wrestling promotion ever staged. It was televised to pay-for-view cable television and to theaters across the country, and staged at sites in Chicago (where I participated), Long Island, and Los Angeles. I was part of a *twenty-man* tag team match, the object being for each contestant to throw the other contestants over the top rope rung and out of the ring.

Chicago's William "Refrigerator" Perry, 300 pounds of nice young man, competed in this event, but his size seemed as nothing compared to wrestler Andre the Giant, seven feet five inches tall and weighing 555 pounds, who ultimately won the match.

Perry reminded me of my younger self: open, innocent, friendly, totally unspoiled. This big defensive tackle had excited the nation, running for touchdowns and even catching a touchdown pass. I had a chance to talk to Perry a few days before the wrestling promotion. I suggested to him that during the coming season he concentrate on football, which brought him his fame in the first place.

Other football players taking part in Wrestlemania II included Jim Covert of the Bears, former Steeler Ernie Holmes, Bill Fralic of the Falcons, and Russ Francis of the Forty-niners. Too Tall Jones had been scheduled to compete, but Cowboy management objected, fearing he might get hurt, and my friend ended up serving as a referee.

Many of the pro wrestlers seemed uptight to me before the match. They thought the football players might try to embarrass them, and they intended to show we were on *their* territory. "I'm going to throw you out of the ring, fat man," snarled Big John Studd at Refrigerator Perry in one of the lighter moods. And he did. But Fridge fooled him. He reached over the top rung to shake Studd's hand . . . and pulled Studd out of the ring! For my own part, as I was in the process of heaving Pedro Morales over the top rope, somehow he managed to take me with him.

I'll say this for the wrestlers: They were very acrobatic and expert at knowing how to fall.

I thought it excellent low humor: George "the Animal" Steele ate a belt buckle. Jake "the Snake" Roberts brought a live python into the ring and proceeded to wrap it around the neck of George Wells. Adorable Adrian Adonis wrestled in a dress, Rowdy Roddy Piper in a kilt, and Uncle Elmer wore bib overalls and nothing else.

A featured boxing match pitted television's Mr. T against Rowdy Roddy Piper. Mr. T won. I knew that earlier, before the fame of "The A Team," he'd worked as Muhammad Ali's bodyguard and had won the nationally televised "Bouncers Tough Man" contest. Mr. T and Hulk Hogan seemed genuinely to love children.

Among the television commentators were Vince McMahon, Susan St. James, and Cathy Lee Crosby. Watergate's G. Gordon Liddy served as a judge.

My being away from football has agreed with me. I continue to work out, keep myself in shape, and today I weigh 245 pounds. I think of Ernie Stautner every time I step on a scale. He put me at the Fat Man's Table, and for years tried to get me down to 252, but except after my jaw operation, when I couldn't eat, I never got to his magic number while on the team.

Friends say I still could play football. I'm only thirty-five years old and, except maybe for that injured right shoulder, which could again be strengthened with the help of someone like Bob Ward, I probably could—physically. Mentally, I still have hurts I can't forget. I know there will be no more football for me, except tossing the ball with Mary's kids.

Like myself, Sharon Bell never married. She keeps in touch, though. In fact, she called just the other day from San Francisco.

"How you doing, Harvey?"

"I'm doing a movie. Finishing my book. I'm telling everybody how you abandoned me."

"Tell them this," she said, laughing. "Tell them you deserved it."

Feeling sweet and sour, I laughed, too.

INDEX